What are people sayir

Introducing You to Your O. ....ccuon

Introducing You to Your Own Perfection is a beautiful blend of philosophical modalities creating a perfect synergy that gives the reader an education for living along with a spiritual map to navigate on this life journey that will lead to joy and peace.
Anita Moorjani, New York Times best-selling author of *Dying to Be Me and What If This Is Heaven?*

With his fascinating book, *Introducing You to Your Own Perfection*, Akash Sky gives us a riveting overview of the modern spiritual masterpiece, *A Course in Miracles*, as well as valuable insights into other related spiritual practices. I was impressed by the uncompromising nature of the teachings herein, and the clarity of how they are presented. I highly recommend this important book.
Gary R. Renard, the best-selling author of *The Disappearance of the Universe* trilogy and *The Lifetimes When Jesus and Buddha Knew Each Other*

Introducing You to Your Own Perfection is a fascinating book that would change your life. Akash Sky takes you on a journey inwards to help remove the Ego – to gain eternal wellness of your being. Highly recommended!
Ravi Bhanot MBE, author of *Everyday Wisdom For All*

Introducing You to Your Own Perfection

A Guide to Walking the Path to Peace with Our Inner Guru

Introducing You to Your Own Perfection

A Guide to Walking the Path to Peace with Our Inner Guru

Akash Sky

Winchester, UK
Washington, USA

JOHN HUNT PUBLISHING

First published by O-Books, 2023
O-Books is an imprint of John Hunt Publishing Ltd., 3 East St., Alresford,
Hampshire SO24 9EE, UK
office@jhpbooks.com
www.johnhuntpublishing.com
www.o-books.com

For distributor details and how to order please visit the 'Ordering' section on our website.

ISBN: 978 1 80341 141 5
978 1 80341 142 2 (ebook)
Library of Congress Control Number: 2022905686

Design: Matthew Greenfield

UK: Printed and bound by CPI Group (UK) Ltd, Croydon, CR0 4YY
Printed in North America by CPI GPS partners

We operate a distinctive and ethical publishing philosophy in
all areas of our business, from our global network of authors to
production and worldwide distribution.

Contents

For Guruji – Who introduced me to my own Perfection.
For Jesus – Who gave us A Course in Miracles.
For Each One of Us, who is part of the Universal Brotherhood
– Home awaits us.

Acknowledgments

I thank the Divine Self for blessing my special relationships and making them Holy.

To my beloved wife Preeti who is pregnant with our second child, I couldn't have done this without you. I am deeply thankful for you letting me have my space to let this book come through into existence.

To our energetic, two-year-old daughter Kyra and all the wonderful things you do. I am blessed to have you.

To Dad, we are not apart.

To Mum for raising me so fondly.

To Maa & Papa, I appreciate all your constant love and support.

To everyone I encounter every day – thank you for showing me what's in my mind.

About the Author

Akash Sky was born as Akash Thapar in South London, England. His career path is Chartered Accountancy where he specialized in Financial Investments. At 30 years old in 2015 he married his wife Preeti in April and moved to North London. That same year in September his dad passed away which was the beginning of his life changing direction. Intense yearning to know who he really is, the meaning of life and his relationship with a greater power followed, and in 2016 he was connected to the essence of Guruji, the Avatar of Hinduism's Lord Shiva, in a formless relationship. That same year Guruji guided him to study *A Course in Miracles* which was dictated by Jesus Christ. Over five years of disciplined self-study internally with Guruji and Jesus Christ, he made many memoirs, notes, and a scrapbook of experiences which led to the existence of this book in 2022.

As this book emerged so did the Akash Sky name. Akash means Sky in the Hindi Language. Akash is the everyday name which represents his personal conceptual self. This self is the temporary individual that will arise through consciousness and dissolve back into it as a projection of the mind. Sky represents the unlimited self. When we look up at the sky we point upwards as if it is there; it is an appearance. Travelling upwards you can't locate it as it has no beginning or end. Its existence isn't the same as objects in our experience such as a car or a chair. You can never pinpoint when you are inside it or when you have made contact with it. There's somehow the joining of both the enormity of outer space with the appearance of a blue dome filled with sunlight. This illusion that something is there is what we call the Sky. In spirituality, the Sky is often referenced because it is equivalent to the inner emptiness or the fullness of ourselves. As we dismantle the Akash personality with Holy Forgiveness it may feel like nothing remains, but this is the beginning of pure existence. *The Sky represents this pure existence and is our inner Perfection.*

Today Akash continues his career in Finance, and is a family man who writes and discusses mystical experiences with other spiritual seekers.

Preface

Our Lives bring us so many obstacles, challenges, and complications. For many, we take the problems at face value and deal with them by giving them power to overthrow our inner peace and Joy. We give away our inner perfection. I wrote this book knowing that it has the potential of changing someone's life. To enable them to be aware that there is a door that can be walked through to inner harmony at every moment. To go beyond our superficial surface mind and connect to the web of all creation. This is a shift in perception, as our interpretation of events opens up to release happiness, freedom and love which can only happen when we know the truth of what we are, where our origin is and how to arrive back at this blissful state. *A Course in Miracles* gives us every possible scenario that blocks us from our divinity. Connecting us directly with our higher self that is an unlimited being, and reversing the effects of our chosen limited conditioning. The course is not the only way, and it might not be the way for everyone, but it will be the way for many, and this book is supportive material to assist anyone wishing for this spiritual transformation.

This book was written under challenging circumstances. It was as if it came out of nowhere, or now-here. Written with the author's higher self who has guided the material throughout in many different surroundings. To name some, stopping the run on the treadmill on countless occasions to write down chapter topics that arise as thoughts, drifting away from conversations with people to go and write down important topics that arose out of words from that conversation, and receiving *A Course in Miracles* words from the texts in the mind to pinpoint what to write in this book. The book began in the UK's national Coronavirus Lockdown, as the writer had an 18-month-old baby, a pregnant wife expecting another, a full-time career

1

outside of writing and a normal householder life with all the regular maintenance to uphold without his wife heavy lifting. The author did not expect a book to emerge from this intense busy period of life. To ensure the message was not lost due to the new baby arriving, it was written during the toddler's naptimes on the weekends and after work hours until late in the week. The intense force inside to get the words down and arrange this material was overwhelming. The desire to assist anyone/everyone and to share the treasure he has found within took over as he wanted to extend his experience and *introduce you to your inner perfection.*

Before I let you in, life was cold and dark.
I was isolated & incomplete, despite life giving me a good start,
There was something missing, I didn't know *"who I am"*,
You came along, with your glorious plan.

I discovered the blocks, the cunning Ego's illusions,
It was me all along, that identified with the delusion.
I ignored you for years, but you never forgot me,
I'm so in debt to you, for setting me free.

I was lost, fragmented & you took me under your wing,
Now not a day goes by where your praises I don't sing.
My life I give to you, as my classroom lesson,
You always take me inward and show me my own Perfection.

Om Namah Shivay, Shivji Sada Sahay,
Om Namah Shivay, Guruji Sada Sahay.
Enormous Gratitude to Guruji & Jesus (Guru-Je)

Foreword

By Anita Kumar
Author of *The Divine Light & Turning The Page*

The force of faith drives our lives whether we are aware of it or not. Everyday life becomes more meaningful when we allow faith to propel us forward as it knows where to take us. Its wisdom is superior to ours and its timing in producing results to our earnest endeavours is impeccable.

Without faith in the universal muscle that holds us together we are likely to sink more than we seek. On us connecting to the supreme power we are able to create a stronger web of like-minded people who walk the path. When we believe, the universe synchronizes occurrences and outcomes that serve the soul.

The soul's journey is to evolve to be better and not bitter. It has chosen to undergo the human experience to clear its karmic account. In doing so it may allow many undesirable situations to enter one's life. The storm may be tempestuous but what tames it is the calmness acquired through faith.

Accepting the storm while striving intelligently to overcome it is what will enable the soul to evolve and scale new heights in the spiritual journey.

I have learnt that the highest form of prayer is a life well lived with joy and gratitude no matter what is served on the plate. Knowing that whatever is happening to us and around us is a consequence of our own actions gives us a sense of ownership. It gives us accountability and we strive to be and do better once we understand that our every action has an equal and opposite reaction. When we have infallible faith in the Supreme power we surrender to whatever is served knowing that He will lighten the load. In this book, *Introducing You to Your Own Perfection*, Akash Sky captures this message deeply.

Introducing You to Your Own Perfection's message throughout is for total surrender to the Divine Being. This rightfully affirms that when we surrender to the Supreme's Divine will He empowers us and encourages us to embark on the journey of enlightenment whereby disperses the life of duality. He dissolves the "I" in us to make us one with Him and that is the eventual goal of every individual. He teaches us that karma is what we live out in our lives; certain occurrences being set in stone, but through our daily prayer, reciting of mantras, loving Him and living in accordance with His will life changes from being sour to supreme. The darkness dissolves to bring in a new dawn. Sky's assured teaching style, attention to detail and clarity of the arguments set out, make this guide one that will intrigue and fascinate the audience. It's a valuable addition to Spirituality.

Belief in the Supreme power makes the rainbow real and the pot of gold at the end of it. Faith fortifies us and we remain unshaken by the unpleasant surprises that life throws at us. Infallible faith becomes the window behind which we stand unaffected both by the scorching heat and the biting frost.

Patience and perseverance, however, are the attributes that forge us ahead on our spiritual journey. Wisdom prevails through our experiences providing we are awake. Awareness is the prerequisite to soul evolvement. Being alone and connecting with that power is what will eventually awaken us to our own truth. It is in stillness and silence that we hear His heavenly word. Hence the noise of the world needs to be mitigated and on doing so the paramount process of detachment takes place.

Consciously finding joy each moment ebbs away sadness and despair. Gratitude spills over and we sip His nectar of love as we allow all that is trivial to slip away. *Introducing You to Your Own Perfection* brings strong awareness in removing blocks to reveal continuous Joy. Akash Sky admirably opens us up to this possibility.

Anita Kumar
Author of *The Divine Light and Turning The Page*
Delhi, India
December 2021

Introduction

Mooji on the purpose of life:

... to be creative, imaginative, to try everything that maya (the great illusion) offers you. Then at some point to even appreciate the wonderfulness of the creative expressions of God but in the end to find that only God is enough. We try everything; it's all temporary and there are no accidents, but the wise ones are tired of experiencing, picking up burdens, tasting this, trying that and finally – feeling blessed have had enough of transient experiences – we turn inward to find the one that never leaves you.

Self-realization is a journey we are all on, whether we recognize it or not. As I gaze my eyes upon the world, I see everyone searching for the same thing. Love, peace and Joy. They look for it in many places but only get diluted experiences. They search for it in food: we all know that first bite of a long-awaited chocolate bar or sweet dessert, it fills us with warmth and satisfaction. However, if we were to eat too much of it then that feeling evaporates and changes to quite the opposite experience. We can also say that we don't really want the dessert or chocolate bar, but we actually want more of the short happy feeling it gives us.

They search for Love, peace, and Joy in fashion, by dressing the body with garments to improve their appearance and give a heightened sense of self. However, new trends emerge, and the clothes become out of date, so they get caught into a cycle of constant maintenance of this self-image which is exhausting to keep up with as the body ages. You can say they don't really want the fashionable garments but actually want the heightened feeling it gives.

They search for it in money, so they can have more options

in life. More money allows more holidays, more cars, more comfort, and special treatment. These luxuries provide them with security and a feeling of safety which leads to temporary peace. You can say they don't really want the money; they want the comfort, safety and peace it brings.

They search for it in power and status: the higher their status and power, the more they are a decision maker and less a servant. Being the decision maker allows them to feel more freedom than a servant would. Freedom to rule with much more choices to choose from. Having freedom gives us the peace, Love and Joy we seek. But in this world this Power and status needs to be earned with endless hours of commitment, networking, extreme hard work, and when you have arrived at where you want to be there's still the protection of your power and status which is so strenuous. Their peace, Love and Joy doesn't last very long. You can say they don't really want power and status, but the freedom it brings.

They search for it in temples, churches, mosques, and synagogues, that loving connection to something greater than them in these holy places. But when they leave the surroundings, they can't sustain the loving connection as it was found to be outside of them not within. You can say they don't really want the holy places, but the feeling that the loving connection brings.

They search for it in sexual intimacy, whether it's a fast intensified orgasm or a longer loving slow moment to extend the temporary happiness. But these moments bring you up only to drop you back down; you can say they don't really want the intimacy, they want the idea of being loved or the climax which takes them away from their world for temporary pleasure.

It seems there is a trend here. We could repeat this for a long while but let me assure you it works for alcohol, drugs, roller coaster rides, friendship, relationships, hosting and attending events, careers, education and all the other ways we try to find Love, peace and Joy in our lives. The truth is, there is no Love, Joy and peace out there in this world if you haven't found it within.

At 30 years of my life, I was living proof that none of that makes you constantly happy. I tried everything and had everything I wanted; searched, and searched for continual happiness but it just never lasted. It came and dissolved like beautiful waves that crashed onto the rocks. It comes in different forms, like I have mentioned, but vanishes as if it never happened and now only lives in my past thoughts. I could have spent the rest of my life trying to find it out there in what we call the world, but sense prevailed, and I went inward instead. After deep self-inquiry I can honestly say I can bring peace, Love and Joy into my life at my will, whenever I desire it and it's not dependent on anything in the world. I don't need food, fashion, money, power, status, holy buildings, sex, alcohol, drugs, roller coaster rides, friendships, relationships, events, careers or education to make me feel temporarily happy, because when I go inward, I know I'm constantly loved, at peace, in Joy and am whole (lacking nothing), innocent, never changing and Eternal.

You may think this is impossible, since it goes against everything the world teaches, but the world is designed to show you what you are not so you can remember what you are. That is **Re-Mind** you that you are part of the one mind, the mind of God. **Forgetfulness** is here **For Getting the Fullness** back of how you were created. You may faintly be able to **Recall** your birth, but this was not the beginning of you, you are now being **Re-called** back to Love. "What am I" is the only question you need to answer, because when you have the answer and live by it, your outside world changes because you perceive everything from an inward state leading to a perception shift where you can choose to only see love and experience peace in every situation.

"How" is surely the next question. Well, I use a tool called *A Course in Miracles*, which connects me with my real state of being by surrendering to the memory of what I am, which the course calls "The Holy Spirit". This can also be known as your higher self from which our intuition is drawn. Because what I am is changeless, it can only be a memory if I had the choice to forget it, but being changeless if I chose to forget it, it doesn't mean I can change what I am. What I am will always be even if I try to overlay it with an idea of me. Like the sun gets covered by the clouds, only some of its rays pass through, but no matter how many clouds are there the sun will always be behind them. If we were to remove the clouds, then we would reveal the sun. Similarly if you were to remove the idea of yourself which you have chosen to cover your real self with, you will experience just how peaceful, loving and joyful this world can be through what you really are.

The course is very simple, but it's not easy. It's simple because at every moment of your life there are only two things to choose from, which teacher do you want to see this particular moment with. Either the memory of what you are (known as The Holy Spirit), or what you think you are (known as The Ego) and it's actually even simpler than that, because the Ego doesn't even exist so there's really only the Holy Spirit. It's not easy because we are entangled within the idea of what we think we are, the self-concept, the person, the "I", the mind construct of an individual which we believe is us. It is not. For example, I think I'm Akash, and everything that he is, is the block to what I really am. By being Akash I've singled myself out from the rest, I've become a fragmented part of the whole and can be observed by the other parts of myself as different to the rest. On a blank white wall can any part blame the other? Can it defend its position? Can it cause suffering to other parts of the wall? It's all the same unified space. Similarly you, I and all the other conscious beings out there are all one appearing as many. The many is an illusion. The course puts it as you are the dreamer of the dream not the dream figure. The real you that is whole, eternal, changeless and complete love is dreaming this entire cosmos and the sleeping fragmented mind has superimposed or limited itself through the median of perception and thoughts.

You think you are these thoughts. You are much, much grander.

Since our mind is conditioned it's covered with fear; that fear is what holds the concept of what we are in place. We need assistance and assistance is here. The course is taught to us by the manifestation of the Holy Spirit, Jesus. For some this will be ideal as he is such a prominent figure in the West, and for others it may be difficult to fully surrender to a symbol which the world has made a bitter idol of. In this situation we would forgive ourself for perceiving him that way, or if it's not working for you still, it is necessary to build a relationship with the Non-Ego part of yourself so another symbol can help. This may be Buddha, Guru Nanak, YHWH, Krishna or anyone else that connects your mind to the Non-Ego Part. I was born into this world as a Hindu, so I use a combination of Jesus and Guruji who is the Avatar of Lord Shiva. I connected to this Guru after he left his body so never met him in person, but after many mystical experiences I have full personal evidence that he is a genuine master. These masters have swum the shores to self-realization and are the *Mastermind* (that is the *Masters-Of-The Mind*). This combination works for me, you will find the best way for you. I may refer to this Guruji-Jesus combination as Guru-Je.

Although the promise is Love, peace and Joy, it's not a better material life. The point is you have the Joy no matter what the circumstance you are in. This isn't the book named the secret, with the law of attraction, we don't want to attract a lovely partner, a new car, a million dollars, a big home, because if we do we are doing this through the Ego and you're back to the first paragraph of this book again. This is about knowing that you don't know what's best for you, but the omnipresent Holy Spirit does know and you continually surrender to it. This is a lifelong commitment and ensures that you build a relationship with the part of you that is eternal as opposed to all other relationships here that are temporary. As we keep overlooking the Ego it eventually fades out of our perception and we are not slaves to its worldly cravings. We become enveloped with the Love of our Creator.

The one purpose of this book is to open the door to freedom for you. *A Course in Miracles* is a three-part book of Text, Workbook Lessons and Teacher's Manual. There's only one rule: don't do more than one workbook lesson a day and there are 365 lessons. You don't even need to buy the book; you can download it for free like I did. If you are part of a particular religion like I am, remember it's a self-study so there's no one to meet up with to chant positive affirmations with, sing hymns or bhajans with, to give charity donations to or holy buildings with statues to pray to as it is not a religion. As Akash I'm still a member of the Hindu community. I'm just much more aware of truth and illusions as the connection to my awakened inner teacher is alive. The course is simply the truth. Your inner guide will translate it all to you. It will connect you to the materials, people or places to go. It's such a wonderful experience. Everything I know has been guided to me by my inner teacher and I extend this to you so we can share our Joy together.

This book begins by explaining how we arrived in this state. Read it with an open mind. It moves into the secret dream to describe the reason why we do the insane things here. It progresses to how we practically deal with every difficult situation by the Holy Spirit's forgiveness. The body and death are large fear barriers to happiness so are next. We move onto understanding just how grand we are beyond Space-Time, with our limited perceptions containing us. We look at the Unified Field which increases our awareness of how everything is connected. The Ego's dynamics are crucial to understand illusions/blockages to our peace and are next. Then we conclude with how it has completely transformed my life from lost to found, from incomplete to full, from loneliness (despite having it all) to contentment – *after all there has only ever been **One** of us, so how can we be L-**one**-ly?*

Chapter One

The Separation from God – the Origin

*– What we call our life is us, the Child of God seemingly **P-laying** on our own away from our Creator. The truth is, we are **Laying** inside of our Creator dreaming of being separate, whilst our Creator doesn't acknowledge us as separate, it holds perfection perfectly in place for us to awaken into itself. –*

At the Beginning & Disconnection from our Source

To extend is a fundamental aspect of God which he gave to his son. In the creation, God extended himself to his creations and imbued them with the same loving will to create. You have not only been fully created but have also been created perfect. There is no emptiness in you. Because of your likeness to your Creator you are creative. No child of God can lose this ability because it is inherent in what he is, but he can use it inappropriately by projecting. The inappropriate use of extension, or projection, occurs when you believe that some emptiness or lack exists in you, and that you can fill it with your own ideas instead of truth. This process involves the following steps:

First, you believe that what God created can be changed by your own mind.

Second, you believe that what is perfect can be rendered imperfect or lacking.

Third, you believe that you can distort the creations of God, including yourself.

Fourth, you believe that you can create yourself, and that the direction of your own creation is up to you.

These related distortions represent a picture of what actually occurred in the separation, or the "detour into fear." None of this existed before the separation, nor does it actually exist now. Everything God created is like Him. Extension, as undertaken by God, is similar to the inner radiance that the children of the Father inherit from Him. Its real source is internal. This is as true of the Son as of the Father. In this sense the creation includes both the creation of the Son by God, and the Son's creations when his mind is healed. This requires God's endowment of the Son with free will, because all loving creation is freely given in one continuous line, in which all aspects are of the same order. (T-2.1.1:1)

I was going to explain the above in my own words, but my inner voice pointed out that a book – *The Disappearance of the Universe* written by Gary Renard – describes it perfectly. This book is outstanding. In the below "Christ" can easily be understood to be "Child" or the "Offspring" of God. If you are of a different religion to Christianity this may not sit well with you, but as mentioned in the Intro, *A Course in Miracles* isn't associated with any religion, Christ is universal, whether Atheist, Buddhist, Muslim, Hindu, Jewish, Christian, Sikh, other – the Child is all of us as one.

The Disappearance of the Universe – Chapter 4, Page 122

Before the beginning, there were no beginnings or endings; there was only the eternal always, which is still there – and always shall be. There was only an awareness of unflawed oneness, and this oneness was so complete, so awe-striking and unlimited in its joyous extension that it would be impossible for anything to be aware of something else that was not itself. There was and is only God in this reality, which we will refer to as heaven.

What God creates in His extension of Himself is called Christ. But Christ is not in any way separate or different than God. It is exactly the same. Christ is not a part of God; it is an extension of the whole. Real love must be shared, and the perfect love that is shared in God's universe is beyond all human comprehension.

13

Humans appear to be part of the whole, but Christ is all of it. The only possible distinction between Christ and God – if a distinction is possible – would be that God created Christ, he is the author, Christ did not create God or itself. Because of their perfect oneness, this doesn't really matter in heaven, God has created Christ to be exactly like God, and to share his eternal love and joy in a state of unencumbered, boundless and unimaginable ecstasy.

As God created Christ in his extension of himself, Christ also has instant extensions that are infinite and everywhere. This everlasting communion between the Father, child and further creations is an eternal breathing in and out of Joy, Bliss and Love. Gary continues now on how we arrived at our state of consciousness:

The Disappearance of the Universe – Chapter 4, Page 123
Then something appears to happen which, as in a dream, doesn't really happen just appears to. For just an instant, for just one inconsequential fraction of a nanosecond, a very small aspect of the Christ appears to have an idea that is not shared by God. It's kind of a "What if" idea, it's like an innocent wondering in the form of a question – which unfortunately is followed by an apparent answer. The question, if it could be put into words was, "what would it be like if I were to go and play on my own?" ... like a naïve child playing with matches who burns down the house you would have been much happier to not find out the answer to that question, for your state of innocence is about to be seemingly replaced by a state of fear and the erroneous, vicious defences that this condition appears to require. Because your idea is not of God, he does not respond to it. To respond to it would be to give it reality. If God himself were to acknowledge anything except the idea of perfect oneness, then there would no longer be perfect oneness. There would no longer be a perfect state of heaven for you to return to. The truth is you haven't really left anyway. You're still there, but

you have entered into a nightmare state of illusion. While you have travelled only in dreams, God & Christ, who are always one, have continued as they always did and always will – completely unaffected by what Jesus refers to in the Course of Miracles as the "Tiny mad idea" of separation.

In this fraction of a nanosecond, it appears that there is now independence. It seems that Christ is now aware of something else. A dream of oneness to duality. That is, dual realities; God and another. This another is an illusion. A distorted dream with continual situations which are symbolic of separation. Without the power of God we can't create in the fullness and natural way we are supposed to. This leads to everything that we make breaking down, and in the end it never works out.

Have no fear, The Voice of God and heaven is still within you, The Holy Spirit. This inner voice is still here to remind you of the truth and call you to return, this fail-safe memory of what you are can never be lost, making an awakening to the reality of heaven completely inevitable.

However, this memory can be seemingly delayed by unwise choices in the dream. Unwise choices have been made by you all along. You have the power to choose the memory and strength of God or something else instead which we call The Ego. If you really examine your thoughts, you will find that you are usually choosing something else instead. That is what part of your mind that chooses did immediately after the seeming separation. Out of shock, fear and confusion it made a series of unwise choices that resulted in you appearing to be here. You still don't realize that given the awesome power of the mind, certain choices made by you could end the seeming separation – and could have at any time. That doesn't mean that it's going to be easy at this point, but it does mean that you are capable of accomplishing it – with some help.

Make no mistake; in order to really accept God's helper, the Holy

Spirit, you must begin to trust God. You cannot trust him until you recognize that it is not him but you who is responsible for your experiences. You will feel guilty until you understand that this world is not real and that nothing has really happened. That doesn't mean you shouldn't act responsibly in the illusion. God could not have created this world, it would not be in his nature, he is not cruel.

When I read the above, I immediately felt the words were true, and I was guided to also read the Bhagavad Gita, chapter 13, which describes our **independence and miscreation.** After reading the below I was astounded at how similar the message was.

Bhagavad Gita: As It Is – Chapter 13, Text 23

The fact is that individual living entities are eternally part and parcel of the Supreme Lord, and both of them are very intimately related as friends. But the living entity has the tendency to reject the sanction of the Supreme Lord and act independently in an attempt to dominate the supreme nature, and because he has this tendency, he is called the marginal energy of the Supreme Lord. The living entity can be situated either in the material energy or the spiritual energy. As long as he is conditioned by the material energy, the Supreme Lord, as his friend, the Supersoul, stays with him just to get him to return to the spiritual energy. The Lord is always eager to take him back to the spiritual energy, but due to his minute independence, the individual entity is continually rejecting the association of spiritual light. This misuse of independence is the cause of his material strife in the conditioned nature. The Lord, therefore, is always giving instruction from within and from without. From without He gives instructions as stated in Bhagavad-gita, and from within He tries to convince him that his activities in the material field are not conducive to real happiness. "Just give it up and turn your faith toward Me. Then you will be happy," He says. Thus the intelligent person who places his faith in the Paramatma or the Supreme Personality of Godhead begins to advance toward a blissful eternal life of knowledge.

We are all searching for the peace, Love and Joy which is the natural state of what we are. Created by perfection we are perfect, whole, complete, and innocent. Our Perfect, all-loving creator created one child in spirit extending itself into Eternity. Spirit is the thought of God which it created like itself. The unified spirit is God's one child. Before time began the one child was curious and wanted to know what it actually felt like to be by itself from the creator. The child wanted to be an "I" to experience itself. This is what *A Course in Miracles* refers to as the "tiny mad idea" or the "detour into fear". God only created an unlimited being, and in order to experience a "self" the being has to fragment into smaller limited parts and be covered or concealed by something else. Like a lit match in front of the sun cannot be distinguished, something else has to arise to present an image. Thus what arose through the child's intense desire to be an "I" was a dream with the Ego thought system. Thankfully God didn't acknowledge us as separated from him, as it would make of our creator an unloving father. Instead, the result was the child fell into a dream with a made-up illusionary thought system which if the child identified with, the child can feel as if it is an "I" or a "self-personality". We should feel very grateful that it's impossible to lose the Voice of God otherwise we would be trapped in isolation in unconsciousness. *A Course in Miracles* calls this the Universal Mind or the Holy Spirit. This voice can be symbolized by many names, Buddha, Krishna, Jesus, Guruji, Guru Nanak, YHWH, which are all the awakened mind. *A Course in Miracles* also describes very clearly that "God doesn't know you are here" and that it didn't create the "world". The child identified with the Ego and is dreaming it. This is how vast and supreme the child has been created. Kenneth Wapnick, by many regarded as one of the best teachers of the course says, "God is like a parent who knows its child is dreaming and having a nightmare but not the content of the nightmare." We can also say God knows that we broke communication with him and are thus experiencing a lack of joy. The constant going out of God's love is blocked when his channels are closed. His love is blocked when the mind he created does not communicate fully with him. This happens when we choose the Ego self which is done when the Mind superimposes limitations through a medium of perception and thought. These limitations can be loosened as we affiliate more and more with our Higher Self – which my chosen symbol Guru-Je (Guruji-Jesus) directly connects me to through daily surrender.

So, this first chapter explains How we got here and also the miscreations we have chosen in order to arrive at this state. The next chapter focuses specifically on Self-Inquiry so we can practically go deeper into what we are.

Chapter Two

Self-Inquiry, You Are Not This Person

*– We have **Overlayed** an image of an individual self on top of the creator's Divine creation, which is the real you. This will be **Over** once you **Lay** this individual image of a self to rest. –*

Advaita Vedanta Self-Inquiry; Pancha Kosha, 5 Sheaths

Let's discuss the "I" or "self-personality". The Ego mind creates bodies and projects them out into a dreamlike world. The Holy Spirit also creates bodies into this world, but these beings are egoless and appear to be very different or not from here because they are from the awakened mind. They come here to assist us to move along the journey. They can be known as Enlightened beings or Spiritual Masters who have walked the earth such as Buddha, Guruji and Jesus. They can also be known as the embodiment of The Christ. It is very important to note here that we will eventually all become Enlightened Masters and if you are looking at this from outside of time, we are all back in oneness with God right now, so it's not only possible, it is already done. It's like the real Child of God is dreaming and seeing a screen of the time space continuum with all the apparent lives of past-present-future and activities occurring through the screen of consciousness; from this view there is only now happening all at once. Only when you are "in" time does there "appear" to be a past, present and future. We will talk about space-time and the dynamics of the Ego later, but effectively you are not the person that you think you are. You are the being inside that is aware of your individualized experience. Let's look at the self-inquiry technique from Advaita Vedanta. The most direct path and the highest of paths in Advaita Vedanta is the analysis of the five layers of the human personality. First revealed in the Taittiriya

Upanishad which was written around 600 BC, this Upanishad is the source material for a detailed analysis of the 5 koshas. It's effortless and the impact is immediate if followed sincerely. Let us take a look at the Pancha Kosha, 5 Sheaths, which are set to encase the true self. This must be understood for liberation and takes you inward to be with your real self:

The First Sheath is Annamaya

The Sheath of the Physical body, the Grossest of the five Koshas. Here we say the body is a product of food, a rearrangement of food. Living through this layer humans identify themselves with a mass of skin, flesh, fat, bones and feces. The Upanishads says let's take a closer look at this, there are lots of disturbing reasons why we are not the body:

Firstly, the same body changes: it was a baby, then a child to adolescence, then an adult and finally to an old body. Were you really the baby? If I was that baby the body certainly is not me. How can I be the body if it is always changing, and I am not?

Secondly, the body is an object, the knower and the known are two different entities. I can smell, taste, see, hear, and feel the body. I am the knower of the body. The body does not know me. I know my foot, my foot does not know me; all body parts can be questioned like this. Remember you sense the body; you look at the body, the body is not doing that to you. You are the seer, the body is the seen.

Thirdly, always we think of ourselves as conscious, the body is something we are conscious of, the body is not conscious of you.

Fourthly, the happiness and misery we are experiencing today is because of the past. The causes must have been there before the body for the effects to come here now; the causes of this must be prior to this body. Karma, cause and effect show us this. There are lots of people who are doing good and bad things in life and do not seem to get the effects in this life. This will happen in the next body after this body has passed. The body does not accompany them after death, so you must be apart from the body. You exist before and after the body. Not only Vedanta says this; all religions tell us there is something else other than the body.

To conclude the real you is something different to the food body known as the Annamaya. Let's look deeper to pranamaya.

The Second Sheath is Pranamaya

Pranamaya is the Energy Sheath, the vital force that enlivens the body. There is oxygen being assimilated into the blood, there is blood flowing through the veins, there is food being converted to energy in all parts of the body; so much is going on. A variety of biochemicals are being produced by the body. All these life processes are flowing through the body all the time that keep our body alive. Our experience of breathing, thirst, sickness, lack of energy is due to prana. Prana is the force that vitalizes the body-mind. The body changes at a slower rate than the prana, which is constantly moving; we are healthy because of the prana not the body. The Chinese call it Chi. Indian medicines which are Ayurvedic try to act on prana and that produces physical health. It can now appear that you are the Pranamaya, but look closer: Is it changing? Yes, sometimes you are energetic, sometimes absolutely dead tired. Sometimes I am sick, sometimes healthy. The prana changes and flows through the body and is continuously changing. I am unchanging, I am the same person who is ill, who is cured but the prana has changed. I am the same person who is hungry and the same who is full, the prana has changed.

To conclude, Prana is known, I am the knower. Prana is a subtle object like the body is an object. You cannot see it but can certainly feel it. It is not you either. Go deeper and look within yourself to Manomaya.

The Third Sheath is Manomaya

Manomaya is the Mind Sheath – thoughts, emotions, the personality, memories, sensations. It is the cause of diversity, of "I" and mine. We think we are our likes, dislikes, thoughts, our identity, our feelings. When commercials are playing and they say "find yourself" they mean your personality, your mind. This is what most adult's think they are and get stuck at. Let us take a look. Are you aware of your mind? When you are sad do you know you are sad? When you have desires do you know you have desires? I want chocolate, am I the desire that wants that object of desire? No, clearly you cannot be the mind. The mind is something that is experienced, just as the body and prana is experienced, the personality is also experienced inside by something greater. I am the seer of the mind and the mind is the object.

The mind is changing continuously. There are thousands of thoughts (mostly repetitive) in a waking day. I am the one to whom these thoughts come. So many desires, but I am one. I am not the mind. Look deeper for something more subtle to Vijnanamaya.

The Fourth Sheath is Vijnanamaya

The Intellect Sheath is the faculty which discriminates, determines, or wills. The abode of your willpower, decisiveness, and Ego. It is endowed with the function of knowledge and identifies itself with the body and organs. The Intellect and mind are the same instrument but performing different functions. The distinction is the intellect understands, and it is also the agent to understanding. When I feel I am speaking it's not the mind, it's the certainty that is within my mind. When I say I do not understand what Akash is saying or I do understand what Akash is saying this is the intellect. Let's apply the same logic. Are we aware of the intellect? Yes. Are we aware if we understand or do not understand something? Yes. If I am aware of it the intellect becomes an object ever so subtle but still an object. It changes all the time. So many things we understood at school and have forgotten. So many things we did not understand in school which we do now, and so many things remain to be understood. I thought I was the same person who knew trigonometry in school and college and not now – I am the same person; the intellect has changed but I am the same.

I am the unchanging witness of the intellect. It's very close to the Atman (the true self). It shines in the light of the Atman but still it borrows consciousness from you, it is not you. Let's look deeper at Anandamaya.

The Fifth Sheath is Anandamaya

Anandamaya – the Bliss Sheath which is the subtlest. When we are in deep sleep we forget the body; if it is a dreamless sleep, there is no intellect in the sleep either. Yet something is there. Something knows you slept peacefully and remembers that you had had no dreams to remember. Not knowing is also knowing. We experience blanklessness or untroubled rest. This sheath is what gives us happiness in the waking state. Also when I bite into a chocolate brownie it's percolated from the Bliss sheath. But this too is an object. It's experienced. Who is the experiencer of this? It changes.

Okay, so if I am not the five sheaths, what am I? The first reaction is I have peeled the onion, or I've opened the Russian dolls and there is nothing inside at the end. It seems this way when it is viewed upon by the finite mind that thinks it knows things, which is only capable of knowing objects. *It is not nothing, it's empty of objects but full of itself.* You are the experiencer, the watcher who is aware of all. It is not an object of seeking. The five sheaths are not objects separate from consciousness; they arise in our consciousness in forms. We do not need to look deep into a flame to know it's fire, or a table to know it's wood, or a puddle to know it's water; it's all consciousness. We are immortal pure infinite existence.

As mentioned earlier, *A Course in Miracles* takes this further with Jesus describing that Spirit being the thought of God, is the only true reality that exists. Jesus says this about consciousness: *"Consciousness, the level of perception, was the first split introduced into the mind after the separation, making the mind a perceiver rather than a creator. Consciousness is correctly identified as the domain of the ego"* (T-3.4.2:1), and actually only oneness with God is real. *"Consciousnesses is the receptive mechanism receiving messages from above and below, from the Holy Spirit or the Ego. Consciousness has levels and awareness can shift quite dramatically but it cannot transcend the perceptual realm, at its highest it becomes aware of the real world and can be trained to do so increasingly, yet the very fact that it has levels and can be trained demonstrates that it cannot reach knowledge."* (C-1.7.3-6) Jesus also says, *"Consciousness is the state that induces action, though it does not inspire it."* (T-1.2.1:8)

As we move inwards through these layers, we are interrogating each of our beliefs. We are effectively separating out the changing parts from the changeless part. This method directs us to what we are. When I first did this, I was astounded at how quickly I could arrive at the emptiness, which is the entry to pure existence. I wanted it more and more, to be able to call it at my will, but there were blockages to this as daily pain arrived in various forms. The following chapter identifies the chief obstruction to peace, the belief in the separation from God. Remember it's a root belief but anything that is believed can be corrected.

Chapter Three

The Secret Dream

*— The Ego **Conceals** what we dream in secret and shows us our problems are outside of us here in this world. It's a **Con** as it **Seals** tight what is hidden in our mind. —*

How we became an Individual

The secret dream is the source of all the Guilt, Fear, and Pain we experience. We have hidden this very well, so this chapter is not going to be the easiest of reads. Take it in, contemplate on it and move through the other chapters to add more context to dealing with this situation. We need to know what the real problem is in order to correct our error. This chapter concentrates on the extent of our unwise choices. We have been constantly choosing something else instead of the memory and strength of God. This has resulted in us appearing to be here.

You may know the movie *The Matrix*. As I go through the secret dream with you, I feel like Morpheus telling Neo that, "you are living in a dream," and you may remember that he can't believe it and initially it leads to him denying it and vomiting. My experience when this came to my realization was met with sweats and a heated body as the Ego thought system is put on the spotlight. It didn't last long. Hold Jesus/Guruji's hand and walk with him through this chapter.

A Course in Miracles describes the primary split mind as between the Separated Mind and Christ's Mind. The secondary split is within the Separated Mind, divided by two directly opposing thought systems: The Ego or The Holy Spirit, where the Holy Spirit is our guide out of the split as we identify with it.

"The term mind is used to represent the activating agent of spirit, supplying its creative energy. When the term is capitalized it refers to

God or Christ (i.e., the Mind of God or the Mind of Christ)." (C-1.1-2) What this means is Mind enables activities to arise and Spirit which is an eternal constant state is all knowing knowledge. The Mind gives rise to output, actions, and movements. The Mind serves the Spirit, supplying its inspired energy. When the Mind is split, we have Consciousness.

Consciousness is the realm of the Ego as it is the Separated Mind. For the first time, in order to have consciousness we had something else to be conscious of. Like pure light doesn't have separated parts, similarly Spirit is in oneness, everlasting and is unchanging, however, for us to appear separate, the split mind supplies spirit with creative energy to enable activities to facilitate movements, change and motion. Also remember the Ego is not real, it's a made-up thought system to experience an "I" in an illusionary state; it's a dream of separation. Within Consciousness (a dream state) there appears to be many minds with many parts separated out and it is here the desire to be an "I" is constantly re-chosen. Our decision-making mind is constantly choosing the Ego which is why we are still here.

Finally, now we can talk about the material world. The moment we chose the Ego – i.e. our decision to be an individual personality – the Ego mind created further a material cosmos to "feel" and "experience" our separated self within Bodies. This is the Space-Time Continuum, or the Cosmos as we experience it. As we entered as a body in the world, we then conveniently chose to forget that we made the decision to choose the Ego, so we believe that we are people living in a world where things are happening to us and we call this our life. We believe this because our Mind is conditioned. I have a little toddler and everything I show her is conditioning her mind – shapes, colors, objects, numbers, letters, animals etc. are all concepts of the Ego which we have all lived by for all of the years we have been here. They are human made-up ideas in order to "live" here and have some apparent order within the Ego's chaos.

The Split Mind known as consciousness has actually projected outwards a continuous series of pictures, and through these streams of images we have a moving picture. The body, the scenery, the objects and other parts all appear to be separate from one another – the appearance of many is a projection of the Split Mind and is **Fulfilled** through its creative energy. *That is our Fullness is Filled with an appearance of separation and division within itself.* Remember everything after the "tiny mad idea" is an illusionary dream. We are the Christ (God's unified Child) appearing as many fragmentated parts.

Ken Wapnick best described the truth as: "We dream the dream; the dream is not dreaming us." I (which is not this person I think is me as Akash) am the dreamer of the dream. Not this dream figure Akash. I did not come into existence because of my parents. I am not who I am today because of my genetic structure or my upbringing. I am not the product of what other dream figures have seemingly done. It's my dream. Shifting metaphors, it's my play, my script, I'm the author. I wrote the play; I gave myself the starring role, I'm the hero of the play. I described very, very clearly what that hero is going to look like. Down to the color of hair, weight, height, eyes, even chose this dimple, what kinds of clothes he wears – I designed everything. It's my show, I'm the producer, writer, director and I'm the star. The whole play revolves around me and I wrote into my script all kinds of characters. Even my parents and everyone else. It's a monumental extravaganza. I did it and there's a figure in this play called Akash and as arrogant as it sounds Akash thinks he's real. He thinks he does things. That's because he forgets he's all made up; the character has no power he's just a character. He reads the lines that have been given him. When he wakes up in the morning and chooses clothes, he thinks he's doing that. It's all been scripted for him.

A close friend of mine recently said to me that they don't really follow the meaning of consciousness. I gave them an example which happened very recently.

I was staying over at my family members' house. I woke up, got out of bed and walked into the bathroom to have a shower. They have a rainfall showerhead fixed onto the wall, and as I turned on the water all of the tiny holes in the showerhead were blocked and the water couldn't come out. Instead it was gushing out of the side. So, I had to turn the shower off as it was leaking onto the floor and ceiling. I stared at the showerhead and there must have been maybe 70 or so little holes which the water is supposed to pass through for you to stand underneath and get the feeling of a rainfall. In order to unblock each hole, I had to rub the minerals off with my finger. I turned the water on and as I went through each hole, water was finally able to pass through each one. As I reached the last hole, I could feel that warm water dropping on my head just like a rainfall. It was all unblocked and functioning like it should be. As I write this now an analogy arrives at my mind. Each hole which the water passes through creates a unique stream of water which gives the illusion that all the water can appear as separated water. This is because there are now parts the water can pass through i.e. holes and now parts water can't pass through. It's obviously still the same water but the appearance is now different. Let's now call the water consciousness. Similarly Consciousness is overlaid or filtered with perception and thoughts which hold bits of mind as separate awareness. Each separate awareness becomes a unique entity by making up names, symbols and emphasizing space from the rest. This carves out a "person" from the whole. In the showerhead the one flow of water creates 70 different streams that move down to feel like continuous rain. Similarly, from one consciousnesses emerges 7 billion separate bodies which appear as private worlds encased and separate from the whole. Like it appears the one flow of water can be

70 individual flows, it also appears that one consciousness can be 7 billion individual "people". From our perspective outside the showerhead, I can understand that the one flow of water is the same separated water flowing out of the showerhead and is just appearing as divided streams because if I were to remove the rainfall head then water would come out in one stream. Similarly from Guru-Je's perspective outside space-time, each person is an emergence from the one consciousness. We are the same. As I removed the blockages from each hole in the showerhead the water was able to flow through and complete its function. In a similar way, when we give our life over to the Holy Spirit it shifts our perceptions and allows True Love to flow through our lives seeing the others as ourselves. The Holy Spirit removes the blockages.

We believe that "life" is happening to us; it's actually coming from us. Our separated mind has carefully chosen a small span of time to create an individualized self to experience body sensations. Not just once, but many times. You have recreated yourself anew hundreds if not thousands of times in many different forms. The mind projects all these dream figures. From a practical perspective past life regression has proven this: Dolores Cannon has 17 non-fiction books spanning 40 years with her outlining transcripts from her sessions with clients who have gone all the way back to oneness with our source. Now let's look at why we keep choosing the Ego thought system here in this world.

The Hidden Dream to Conceal our Decision-Making Mind

Jesus tells us this in *A Course in Miracles* (T-27.7.11-12):

> *The gap between reality and dreams lies not between the dreaming of the world and what you dream in secret. They are one.*

In other words, there is no Gap between mind and body as the body is a projection from the mind. We are dreaming one dream but from where we are we need to understand it in two parts: the world's dream and the secret dream. The dreaming of the world is the body and its everyday affairs, and the secret dream is the mind, but they are both still the dream state. You do not awaken after your life ends as the secret dream which is hidden still lives on in a seemingly separated mind. So we are still asleep when we leave this body. The actual Gap is between dreaming and awakening in the real world. The real world is the oneness with our source of creation.

> *The dreaming of the world is but a part of your own dream you gave away, and saw as if it were its start and ending, both.*

The start of the world's dream is the secret dream, and the ending of the world's dream is in the secret dream i.e. in the decision-making or dreaming mind. The only difference is the body has covered the secret dream with a mask, a veil, a camouflage so that you can't see that you are a decision-making mind. You can choose again: if you choose the Holy Spirit with its forgiveness at every so-called "problem" in your life you are taking your dream back and clearing the path to awakening at each moment you forgive.

Yet was it started by your secret dream, which you do not perceive although it caused the part you see and do not doubt is real. How could you doubt it while you lie asleep, and dream in secret that its cause is real.

Our universe was created to keep the secret dream hidden, the guilt from "seemingly" choosing to destroy God, to being your own God and being an individual "person" separate from God. This caused too much suffering within the mind, so we projected the guilt onto everything else. It's now not our problem but it's out there. It's the boss who hates me, the toaster that burnt toast, the hose pipe that leaked everywhere, the person who assaulted or abused me, the government who imposes restrictions on me, the parking fine I apparently got, the friend that betrayed me, the husband that left me, the thief who stole my car, the house move that never worked out, the waiter that was so rude to me – all of life is a reenactment of the feeling we felt when we separated from God. The waiter that was rude separated me apparently from my happiness, the parking fine apparently separated me from money, the government restrictions seemingly separated me from my freedom, the house move that fell through separated me from that new home I really wanted – all of these are lies to keep the secret dream hidden, so you blame, attack, judge and condemn the other and keep the separated mind active. We are so mindless that we cannot see the Ego trick, so focused on the problem at hand that we have no chance in seeing the master illusionist's hoax. Judging creates more "time" for you to go through it again which the Ego creates as a different form, so if I blame the waiter and condemn him what happens is the separation appears in another way, maybe my TV stops working, or my boiler breaks down or even my child behaves rudely towards me – Jesus says that there is no hierarchy in illusions, they are all the same thing, a lie. You then choose again to attack or forgive. Of course, I don't mean forgiving in the Ego's way where we make one party guilty and the other innocent. We forgive the waiter for what he has not done and forgive ourselves for choosing the wrong teacher when space-time was projected outward. We are all innocent, whole and spirit, and this situation is not true.

We (the child) did not agree to the Ego to only have suffering here in this "world" which is the obvious outcome to not being with God who is Love. So, it built in bits of pleasure to gloss over the guilt. The pleasure is just shadows of the Joy of what we are in Spirit (our natural state). The food, the entertainment, the hobbies, the events, the holidays, the career successes, the achievements are all there with pleasure and pain built into the system. In fact, when you study *A Course in Miracles* deeply you see that there is no difference between pleasure and pain; they are both here to make you feel like the body is real. It's not, it's an illusion. All pleasure is outside the self, but Joy is within. It's pleasure I get when I cuddle my child, it's not Joy. It's pleasure I get when I eat my favorite food, it's not Joy. It's pleasure I get when I get a job promotion, or someone compliments me or my home or anything in Akash's "life". It's pleasure because it is temporary. It doesn't last. However, Joy is the changeless immortal presence we feel when we actually know we have been created perfect, that we are loved unconditionally and that in truth we are sinless outside of time. We should be so grateful that this is all a lie, and that our home awaits us. The course continues:

A brother separated from yourself, an ancient enemy, a murderer who stalks you in the night and plots your death, yet plans that it be lingering and slow; of this you dream. Yet underneath this dream is yet another, in which you become the murderer, the secret enemy, the scavenger and the destroyer of your brother and the world alike. Here is the cause of suffering, the space between your little dreams and your reality. The little gap you do not even see, the birthplace of illusions and of fear, the time of terror and of ancient hate, the instant of disaster, all are here. Here is the cause of unreality. And it is here that it will be undone.

Jesus cuts right through the lies to the truth. First he discusses the **World's dream**:

The murderer who stalks you in the night and plots your death yet plans that it be lingering and slow; of this you dream.

This is what we all live our lives by. The Murderer is the Ego's version of God. After all, we all believe God takes us away from our "life", we are all going to die a long slow death, at 50, 70, maybe 100 years, but we know how it's going to end. We think that life starts and ends here, but all of mind is the dream state and that includes the body.

He now moves into detailing the **Secret dream**. Open your mind for this is the core of all pain and suffering. At first it wasn't easy for me to take in because we are not in touch with it. It was the toughest part of the course for me, but I assure you the solution was put where the problem lies as we will see in later chapters:

Yet underneath this dream is yet another, in which you become the murderer, the secret enemy, the scavenger and the destroyer of your brother and the world alike.

He means I believe I am the sinner and I destroyed heaven, and since the Ego's thought system always demands punishment, we then become afraid of the punishment that we believe is inevitable and deserved. That we deserve to be punished by the Ego's version of God. Since the collection of thoughts is so horrific and so fraught with pain, the Ego counsels us that we can be free of the guilt and escape the terror of his version of God by leaving the Mind, making up a world and hiding in that world. Specifically, we will hide our thought system, our image of ourselves, in a body. This is the beginning of the World's dream, where in it I am going to blame everyone in my life so God will penalize them and not me. **No one is in touch with that, it's dreamt in secret.** We are in touch with the world's dream, which is you are doing this to me, and the secret dream, where I tried to overthrow God, lies buried and hidden. If I'm not aware of it, I can't change it because I think these problems are happening to me, that the abuser did that to me, that the teacher was prejudiced towards me, the "difficulties" are all happening to me. In the secret dream we deep down believe we destroyed God, that we have been outcast from our home, that we were perfect eternal and everlasting but now homeless and little. Being separated parts now within consciousness we believe we can destroy the other parts of ourselves to try to win over God's love and acceptance, i.e., we can all blame each other. The next time you are about to blame someone remember to feel the pain; don't identify with the pain to be caused by them. Know it's there because I chose the wrong teacher, and follow forgiveness which is in Chapter 4. Blaming them is a lie. The Ego's advice is a lie. God loves its one child unconditionally; our home awaits us if we simply choose it through forgiveness. Our belief in this secret dream is deeply conditioned within our mind, firmly rooted, and sustained by lots of fear levels. For example, we may have a family, a child, a wife or husband, parents, a career, a home with bills to pay, a life with friends, status and apparently a bright future. Having these attachments keeps us mindless so we don't go inwards to tackle the secret dream. Instead, we become entangled, frightened children who feel lack and emptiness from believing the Ego's lies, and now are slaves to keep what little we have. Even if you're a millionaire it's not even slightly close to being everything.

This mindless hiding place we call "life" is a camouflage to conceal the pain of separation. Your life will show you this as day by day it passes by, and you will not be able to hold any of its activities in your hands to keep forever. My child will get married, my wife or husband will separate from me some way either through divorce or apparent death, my parents will follow suit, my career will fade as I retire, the home will need downsizing and my large status and friends group will cease to be as they all exit the world one by one. You will look back on life and know it was a dream. But why didn't I forgive? Why did I protect it all and attack the apparent villains? There are no villains and victims. There is only your beloved brother (another part of me) here to show you the secret dream in your mind so you can forgive it and go back home to peace and joy together. Be grateful for the attacker, for you put them there, so you can say, "This is not true, I know they are God's child and so am I, it's a lie." Be grateful they are showing you what is in your mind so it can be healed by the Holy Spirit. Any feeling of pain or discomfort, whether is subtle like my child breaking my glasses, more serious like having a car accident, or a huge tragedy like a home being burnt down all appear to be varying forms of this root problem, the belief in the separation from God. The cause is this belief and not my child snapping the glasses, the other driver hitting me, or the villain burning my house down; this is the Ego trick. We are dreaming a nightmare because we think we have left our creator who is the source of Love.

Here is the cause of suffering, the space between your little dreams and your reality. The little gap you do not even see, the birthplace of illusions and of fear, the time of terror and of ancient hate, the instant of disaster, all are here. Here is the cause of unreality. And it is here that it will be undone.

All suffering begins here, in the secret dream, or shall I say the decision maker's decision to choose the secret dream. This is so simple, the here being the mind's decision to sleep and dream a dream of separation, sin, guilt, and fear. It will not be undone in the world, it will be undone in the mind. Suffering is not in the things of this world. It's not in an atomic bomb, a virus, an abuse, a hurricane, a car accident, a traffic jam, a murder – it's in the mind that needs to be corrected.

So, this is why we do not want to go home to the everlasting peace. Let's put this simply. We have made ourselves afraid of God and afraid of going back home and have blocked love out. It may not feel that way here, but that's on the surface. When there's a problem we tend to say, "God knows," or "Why did God do this to me," or "I must have done something really bad to have deserved this." God doesn't know because he did not make this world. God isn't doing this to you, you have set this whole situation up yourself. You have not sinned; you have made an error in a dream by choosing the Ego as your teacher and being misguided. Errors can be corrected by choosing the Holy Spirit. In fact the error has already been corrected: outside of time you and your creator are there in oneness. There is the option to delay this peace, but why suffer when there is no need to?

Chapter Four

The Holy Spirit, The Miracle & Forgiveness

*– Holy **Forgiveness** is **For-Giving** the Miracle to another part of yourself to enable all of yourself to be unified. –*

Recapping the previous chapter. When something bad seems to happen to me and I have a feeling emerging to the surface that isn't nice, it's a reenactment of the feeling I felt when I realized I had given up all of Heaven to be this little person. I know the cause isn't here, it all stems from not being with my creator. Without food you'll starve, without water you'll thirst, without an all-loving God there's no life.

Going through the 5 Sheaths is a great way to experience what you are. Notice once you are there it's so peaceful, nothing can hurt it, change it, improve it or destroy it. Also notice we have covered it over with so many layers to not experience it, to hide it. The entire world outside is designed so you don't go inwards for this Joy and Peace, but now you have found this treasure you will want access to it all of the time. To arrive at this state our mind needs to be unwound back through the conditioning we have received all of our lives. Effectively it's relinquishing our Ego entirely. This is a lifelong process and studying *A Course in Miracles* with Guru-Je will accomplish this, but the way it's done is through forgiveness and unwavering trust for the part of you that isn't the Ego. We can't just forgive here and there, but every single moment you feel slight unhappiness. Let's go through what Christ, The Holy Spirit and Guru-Je is.

The Christ, the Holy Spirit, Jesus & Guruji

The Christ:

The course describes Christ as God's Son as he created Him. The complete Son of God, his one creation, his Joy, eternally like God and in oneness with Him. The Course references Christ as a son, but this is gender neutral as Christ is not a body. The course calls us by the name "Christ" but this is not a religious label, and this course is not Christianity. To this point we could simply describe it as we are the child of God, the offspring of the one creator. It is a name given to represent our true Self which we all share, unifying us with one another, and with God as well. It is the Thought which still abides within the Mind that is its Source. The child has not left its holy home and it has not lost the purity in which it was created. It stands unchanged forever in the Mind of God and guarantees that separation is no more than an idea which we have made up. Christ is the connection that keeps us one with God, and gratefully God's will guarantees this state stays eternal always.

Your mind is part of his, and his is of yours. In his part, God's solution rests; where all outcomes are already made, and dreams have ended. He is unaffected from what the body perceives in our world. Home of the Holy Spirit, and at home in God alone, does Christ remain at peace within the Heaven of your Holy Mind. This is the only part of you that has reality in truth. The rest is dreams. Yet if these dreams are given to Christ, they will fade before His glory and reveal to you your holy Self, the Christ. (W-PII.6:3)

The Holy Spirit:

Our creator also created the Holy Spirit, which creates with God and in his resemblance. The Holy Spirit is immortal and changeless. He is the Voice for God. The Holy Spirit gives us the solution to the separation and brings the plan of undoing the

Ego to us. Our particular part in it has been established by the Holy Spirit and it shows us exactly what our part is. Jesus's part was finished perfectly so he has been recognized as the leader in carrying out the Holy Spirit's plan. All power is hence given to him, and he will share it with you when you have finished your part.

The Holy Spirit is described as the remaining Communication Link between God and His separated Sons. In order to fulfill this special function the Holy Spirit has assumed a dual function. He knows because He is part of God; He perceives because He was sent to save humanity. He is the great correction principle; the bringer of true perception, the inherent power of the vision of Christ. He is the light in which the forgiven world is perceived; in which the face of Christ alone is seen. He never forgets the Creator or His creation. He never forgets the Son of God. He never forgets you. And He brings the Love of your Father to you in an eternal shining that will never be obliterated because God has put it there. (C-6.3.)

The Holy Spirit abides in the part of your mind that is part of the Christ Mind. He represents your Self and your Creator, Who are One. He speaks for God and also for you, being joined with Both. And therefore it is He Who proves Them One. He seems to be a Voice, for in that form He speaks God's Word to you. He seems to be a Guide through a far country, for you need that form of help. He seems to be whatever meets the needs you think you have. But He is not deceived when you perceive your self entrapped in needs you do not have. It is from these He would deliver you. It is from these that He would make you safe. (C-6.4.)

In the world you are the manifestation of the Holy Spirit. For me the best way to understand the Holy Spirit is it mediates between illusions and truth. He bridges the gap between dreams and reality where perception leads to knowledge through grace which God has given to him. Since we all have differing perceptions, it meets us where we are and reconciles us back to truth. The Holy Spirit is our way back home, it provides the path which leads us to truth by dispelling dreams. Its goal is the end of dreams, at this end the Voice is then gone. He no longer takes form but returns to the eternal formlessness of God.

Jesus, Guruji or other manifestations of the Holy Spirit:
In the course, Jesus is the manifestation of the Holy Spirit. Jesus does not belong to a particular religion or organization. Jesus is the name of a man who saw the face of Christ in everyone and remembered God, in fact he leads the way for us to arrive back to God. In his vision he became identified with Christ, a man no more, but instead at one with God. The man was a dream figure, as he seemed to be a separate being, walking on his own, inside a body that appeared to contain his self from Self, as all illusions show. Jesus is our rescuer as he was able to see the false and reject it as untrue and Christ required his form so he can appear to us all and save us from our own illusions.

It's not necessary to have a personal relationship with Jesus, although it can be helpful. It is necessary, however, to develop a relationship with the Non-Ego part of you and we don't want to say you won't be saved unless you choose Jesus. That said, if you're born in the Western world it is nearly impossible not to have some sort of relationship with him, as a Christian, a Jew, a Hindu, a Muslim, or atheist. He's such a famous symbol that he's in everyone's mind whether they believe in him or not. Some bitter idols have been made of him in the world. It's for us to forgive him our illusions, and behold how dear a brother he would be to you as he will set your mind at rest at last and carry it with you to God.

Is he God's only Helper? No, indeed. For Christ takes many forms with different names until their oneness can be recognized. But

Jesus is for you the bearer of Christ's single message of the Love of God. You need no other. It is possible to read his words and benefit from them without accepting him into your life. Yet he would help you yet a little more if you will share your pains and joys with him, and leave them both to find the peace of God. (C-5.6.)

For me, as a British Indian born Hindu, I already have a guru as a manifestation of the Holy Spirit, his name is Guruji. Guruji was the one who guided me to the course because I had a constant yearning to realize my true self. So I use a combination of Jesus and Guruji as my Gurus (teachers)/ elder brothers/guides to this realization of self. Deep respect, love, admiration, and gratitude are given to these masters who have completely shifted my perception over the years. Remember they are the Christ, along with you. They will remain with you to show the path from the hell we made to God. When you join your will with them, your sight will be their vision, as the eyes of Christ are shared. Walking with them is just as natural as walking with a brother whom you knew since you were born, actually that is what their relation to you is, siblings created at the same instant by our creator. They are elder because they awakened ahead in time and are here now to join with for our own awakening.

Guruji doesn't have a teaching, he gives holy experiences to all that connect to him. He doesn't have scriptures, and when living here, like Jesus, was a miracle creator on all levels. After Guruji laid his body aside is when I connected to him, and since then mystical experiences occur all the time (many living miracles too) as he organizes and orchestrates my life, brings back my holy mind, and we have honestly laughed together at some of the world's illusions that he reveals to me through my personal perception. As Jesus takes over with Christ Control, Guruji looks for total surrender into the divine light – it's the same connection, the same Christ, us all together as the one perfect child of God.

The Miracle

The traditional miracle, in our world, is performed by a miracle worker, and that person is doing remarkable events in the physical world that are impossible to ordinary physical law, releasing people from conditions which seems like a permanent change. The miracle in the course is much more psychological than this. The Miracle is a shift in perception that happens inside of us. The Holy Spirit comes through me, and I extend forgiveness to you in a way that sets you free, not so much physically but sets you free from psychological chains. The miracle worker sets free the chains from people everywhere they go, and it may heal them physically or the chains may not be noticeable. The result is from the extension of forgiveness which releases the guilt from the separation from God, and in doing that I will see a more whole self in me which the course says I was always all along. I just didn't know it as it was covered over. It's about releasing others and transforming our self-perception by releasing people from the inside.

The Miracle is where I step out of space-time and hit upon that which is eternal, where duality ends. This introduces me to my own eternity. Then I see you are an eternal being and therefore our different opinions don't affect us, and I meet you there to remove the differences that appear to be so. We perform miracles every time we forgive through the Holy Spirit. When we follow *A Course in Miracles* we basically become a miracle worker, not as an achievement, nor as a magician, but as an expression of love that may or may not have observable effects. The Miracle is the only tool we have for controlling time; only revelation transcends it having nothing to do with time at all. Revelation is God revealing knowledge of Himself through direct, wordless, imageless experience of union with Him. This may or may not happen in this lifetime. It could well be the case that you received this previously or will do so in the next life.

The Holy Spirit is the mechanism of miracles. He recognizes both God's creations and your illusions. He separates the true from the false by his ability to perceive totally rather than selectively. A Miracle is really an intervention. They intervene for your holiness and make your perceptions holy. By placing you beyond the physical laws, they raise you into the realm of celestial order. In this order you are perfect. (T-1.1.38:1)

It's important here to realize that the Holy Spirit inspires all miracles because it understands how to maximize Love from within you. As we practice forgiveness repeatedly, we begin to create a state of miracle readiness. This is where we almost immediately forgive the person or situation. In doing this we do not delay Joy or prolong suffering. We can perceive ourselves and the other as infinite being. The World will tell us there are levels or difficulty to miracles but Jesus explains, *"There is no order of difficulty in miracles. One is not 'harder' or 'bigger' than another. They are all the same. All expressions of love are maximal."* (T-1.1.1:1) This means if we are forgiving what appears to be an entire war between nations or my washing machine leaking all over the kitchen, the love is still maximal. Although appearing as different forms there's only one problem, the belief in the separation from God and its being played out here as problems in life. The Ego will show us these issues as external from you and separate from you so you don't identify with its true cause. The miracle establishes that you dream a dream and its contents are not true. Forgiving murderers, global viruses, large corporations, versus seemingly smaller problems like my toast being burnt or a mouse in my house, are all the Ego illusions of creating levels of suffering. These levels allow us to dismiss the smaller issues as trivial, and bring doubt into larger issues that feel difficult to be corrected. In doing this we do not fully forgive, and the separated mind survives and follows us through this life, and appears in different forms later. If not resolved it continues after the body dissolves to keep active the desire to be separate from God. How can there be levels of suffering when we allow some and not others? It's all a lie, God didn't create any suffering whatsoever.

Jesus says, *"The miracle is a learning device that lessens the need for time. It establishes an out-of-pattern time interval not under the usual laws of time. In this sense it is timeless."* (T-1.1.46) So time is reduced because we have forgiven the situation for what it really is and don't need to go through that part of guilt again. We don't need more time to understand what is really happening here, and time becomes redundant when all the guilt is released. *"When you return to your original form of communication with God by direct revelation, the need for miracles is over."* (T-1.1.47:1)

Forgiveness

Forgiveness to destroy – i.e. what forgiveness is not:

Growing up as a child I was always very boisterous and cheeky, I was always testing my parents' and teachers' patience which led me to understand the world's version of forgiveness very quickly. Speaking back, staying out past curfews, questioning rules and fussy habits meant that either I felt like the victim or the villain in many circumstances. Being told to apologize and say sorry was regular feedback from my authoritative figures but I also felt like the innocent one bullied at times. This is a very common experience in our childhoods. Forgiveness to destroy is the Ego's version of forgiveness. It says you have actually done this to me, you have hurt and upset me so much, and you are guilty for that. Now I have experienced the pain you have caused I am finally over it and can forgive you for the way you have acted. This can be for anything, and the Ego creates lots of levels of its forgiveness. At infant school when

I pushed another child down the slide and she fell on her face my teachers made me apologize for causing pain to her and I certainly felt guilty. At primary school I hid a boy's shoes in the toilet because he said mean things to me in the playground; I was forced to apologize and I felt very guilty. At high school my close friend stole sweets from the store and left me in the shop to take the blame; I felt very innocent and made him very guilty. These scenarios appear to be softer forms of the ego's forgiveness; the harder forms are what the world calls crimes, assaulting someone, breaking, entering and stealing valuable possessions, and physical abuse where the Ego has selected out whether you are the villain or victim. We go through life eventually forgiving the other for what they have done to us. The problem here is this makes the separation real; it reinforces the fact that we are both different and separate from each other. It doesn't undo the error, it makes the error real, reinforces guilt and makes us attack further, as you will do to others what you believe has been done to you. The course would put this as it Establishes sin as real and then pretends to forgive it. This is what the world has always blessed, to forgive but don't ever forget. This is a lie.

The Holy Spirit's forgiveness:

The course is clear that we are to Forgive someone for what they have not done. This is not understood from the point of view of the body. It is only understandable from the point of view of the mind. People hurt and upset others; their actions which come from thoughts also hurt people, but on the level of the mind no one has the power to affect the peace and love which God has given us. I am the ruler of the universe, the child of God and no one can take that away from me. When I get angry, upset or hold a grievance on another what I am saying is what you have done to me is so awful, and because of this I will never feel this love again, but it's a lie and is untrue. Said another way, I am giving something outside of me the power to take away my peace, Love and Joy. I'm giving my power away to you, and you control the way I feel and my state of mind. I am the slave, and what is outside of me is the master. The Holy Spirit will say you may have affected my body, my family, my homeland but not my mind. Jesus says to always be vigilant of the kingdom only. You have to catch yourself feeling annoyed and in pain. That's the Ego; don't dive into it, forgive it. Forgiveness is looking at everyone with Christ vision who sees everyone as the same because at the level of the mind we are all the same. You have the same Ego that I do, the same Holy Spirit that I do and the same power to choose between them that I do. Although our bodies may be different, our skin color, our languages, our sexual preferences, our opinions, our religions, our sport rivalries, we are still all the same. This is fact. We are perfect oneness, but it can't be expressed here in this world. However, what can be reflected here that we are all the same.

What do we forgive:
We forgive any kind of an upset; from a mild discomfort to rage and anger, these are warning signs. All upset tells us that our hidden Guilt is rising to the surface from our unconscious mind. We have projected the guilt onto the symbol in front of us, whether a person, an object or an event. I actually thank the symbol for showing me the guilt in my mind so I can release it. Otherwise if I blamed the person or image I would have to go through it again in another scenario or scene pictured by the Ego, because it would not have been released. The Ego wants to bring distance in between yourself and the guilt, and any suitable person, object or event who appears in front of you will do. It wants you to see the guilt outside of yourself by projecting the reason for it into an illusionary person or image. Remember this is just a dream. It's not really happening to you, because the dream figure is not you, it's a character in a play which you can

step back and watch with our inner Guru. The purpose of time is to forgive; that is the only viable answer to life.

3 step approach to How do we Forgive:

Firstly, remove all Judgments and Condemnation.

To Forgive through the Holy Spirit, we do not judge and condemn anyone, this includes ourselves. The truth is, judgment is impossible; we are really giving up what we think we know about judgment and being very honest with ourselves. Let's see what Jesus says about judgment in the course:

> It is necessary for the teacher of God to realize, not that he should not judge, but that he cannot. In giving up judgment, he is merely giving up what he did not have. He gives up an illusion; or better, he has an illusion of giving up. He has actually merely become more honest. Recognizing that judgment was always impossible for him, he no longer attempts it. This is no sacrifice. On the contrary, he puts himself in a position where judgment-through-him rather than by-him can occur. And this judgment is neither "good" nor "bad." It is the only judgment there is, and it is only one: "God's Son is guiltless, and sin does not exist."
>
> The aim of our curriculum, unlike the goal of the world's learning, is the recognition that judgment in the usual sense is impossible. This is not an opinion but a fact. In order to judge anything rightly, one would have to be fully aware of an inconceivably wide range of things; past, present and to come. One would have to recognize in advance all the effects of his judgments on everyone and everything involved in them in any way. And one would have to be certain there is no distortion in his perception, so that his judgment would be wholly fair to everyone on whom it rests now and in the future. Who is in a position to do this? Who except in grandiose fantasies would claim this for himself? Remember how many times you thought you knew all the "facts" you needed for judgment, and how wrong you were! Is there anyone who has

not had this experience? Would you know how many times you merely thought you were right, without ever realizing you were wrong? Why would you choose such an arbitrary basis for decision making? Wisdom is not judgment; it is the relinquishment of judgment. Make then but one more judgment. It is this: There is Someone with you Whose judgment is perfect. He does know all the facts; past, present and to come. He does know all the effects of His judgment on everyone and everything involved in any way. And He is wholly fair to everyone, for there is no distortion in His perception. Therefore lay judgment down, not with regret but with a sigh of gratitude. (M-10.2:1)

Secondly, what to say and keep it Silent in your mind.

There's no need to speak out loud and go up to people and tell them you are forgiving them for what they haven't done. Remember the Holy Spirit's forgiveness is beyond the body and focuses on the mind. Besides the other person being utterly confused as to what you are saying, it's also getting closer to Ego Forgiveness territory when we involve the body.

If forgiveness is related to another person, I say quietly within my mind:

You are innocent, whole and spirit, all is forgiven, and all is released. I'm innocent whole and spirit, all is forgiven and all is released. The separation from God never occurred and we are both in perfect oneness with Father eternally. I chose the wrong teacher to have perceived this, I now choose the right teacher, I choose Guru-Je (or the Holy Spirit).

Of course, if it's more comfortable you can interchange Guru-Je to your preferred Non-Ego part of you in Jesus, Buddha, Krishna, Guru Nanak, YHWH etc.

If I'm forgiving an object within a situation, like my washing machine leaking all over the kitchen floor, a penalty fine received, a delivery of a product bought that has broken pieces, the house boiler breaking down etc. then I forgive myself and leave the first sentence off from the above.

Thirdly, know you are not a body, and neither are they. There's nothing so blinding as perception of form.

This for me was the hardest learning, after 30 years of constant mind conditioning, from nursery to primary school, secondary school, sixth form (high school), university and careers. We are obviously taught that we are people and the body makes us these people, just like when we see a necklace or a ring we focus on these names but forget the substance is gold. Adam, Emily and Priya are names of people but the substance is the being inside. We know that a body is not something I am, it's something I can have and have had many times. This lesson takes much determination, prayer and surrender to master especially when the apparent villain (or victim) is right in front of you or the mind is firmly fixed on the person. We must loosen our ties to our own body and slowly detach from the "self-personality". *Through the Guru's vision we are taught that the other person isn't there, but what you see is a picture of yourself, a **mirror Reflection, so this situation is a gift to enable Reflection on what has appeared to happen** – your own unconscious Guilt of separating with God, projected onto an illusionary person.* The Ego wants to see you as separate from this person so you can attack or defend your self-created image. Hold back your defenses and attacks, be still in the mind, know this is not happening to you but coming from you, and forgive it in your mind silently. I must admit sometimes it's so difficult you're grinding your teeth, but think of your Guru-Je and most importantly think of how your Guru-Je took you in and was completely nonjudgmental to you with all your apparent mistakes. Forgive them for what they have not done, the way he has forgiven you.

I also struggled with behaviors: once I have forgiven in the mind how do I behave with them after? They have just shouted and sworn at me. Jesus says to overlook the error and not make it real. You wouldn't swear back if you knew the body figure isn't there, you wouldn't defend your position either. It is best for you to consult your inner Guru who will lead you to how to behave; mine told me to say something like, "Calm down, it will be alright." Of course, if you are in a violent or dangerous situation do what you must do to get out, contact the authorities and do what is necessary in the world, but remember to forgive and release it eventually. It may have appeared to have happened, the body may have been hurt but you are not the body and neither are they; you are forgiving yourself for what has not happened. In graphic, violent, abusive situations we need to go through all the emotions that surface and deal with them the way we need to. If counselling and psychotherapy is needed then do what you must, but always seek your inner teacher first for counsel who will guide you to the people and places, and will direct you in what to say. In the end, make sure you forgive them and yourself. When I feel attacked, either physically or emotionally, I always remind myself that this is how I felt when God didn't grant my request to be a separate person. After believing the Ego I attacked and hated God (well I tried to, it's impossible to do this really) and wanted to be my own God and make my own Kingdom – which is what we are all doing here everyday. The body in front of me is a reminder of this and an opportunity to release it and be one step closer to going back home forever. Some villains are harder to forgive than others but the longer you wait to forgive the more you suffer. Why delay the peace, Love, and Joy? It's your choice.

Defenselessness

Let's look at some parts of Workbook Lesson 153, *In my defenselessness my safety lies*, so we can remain still when the wave of attack arrives from the Ego and you feel you need to defend your Ego Self-Image. If you do not defend it and do this consistently, you are stating that the Ego is not there, and thus clearing the way to the pure Love and Joy of what you are.

You who feel threatened by this changing world, its twists of fortune and its bitter jests, its brief relationships and all the "gifts" it merely lends to take away again; attend this lesson well. The world provides no safety. It is rooted in attack, and all its "gifts" of seeming safety are illusory deceptions.

It attacks, and then attacks again. No peace of mind is possible where danger threatens thus.

The world gives rise but to defensiveness. For threat brings anger, anger makes attack seem reasonable, honestly provoked, and righteous in the name of self-defense. Yet is defensiveness a double threat. For it attests to weakness and sets up a system of defense that cannot work. Now are the weak still further undermined, for there is treachery without and still a greater treachery within. The mind is now confused and knows not where to turn to find escape from its imaginings.

It is as if a circle held it fast, wherein another circle bound it and another one in that, until escape no longer can be hoped for nor obtained. Attack, defense; defense, attack, become the circles of the hours and the days that bind the mind in heavy bands of steel with iron overlaid, returning but to start again. There seems to be no break nor ending in the ever-tightening grip of the imprisonment upon the mind.

Defenselessness is strength. It testifies to recognition of the Christ in you. Perhaps you will recall the text maintains that choice is always made between Christ's strength and your own weakness, seen apart from Him. Defenselessness can never be attacked, because it recognizes strength so great attack is folly, or a silly game a tired child might play, when he becomes too sleepy to remember what he wants.

Today our theme is our defenselessness. We clothe ourselves in it, as we prepare to meet the day. We rise up strong in Christ, and let our weakness disappear, as we remember that His strength abides in us. We will remind ourselves that He remains beside us through the day, and never leaves our weakness unsupported by His strength. We call upon His strength each time we feel the threat of our defenses undermine our certainty of purpose. We will pause a moment, as He tells us, "I am here."

I remember when my first baby was born, I was so excited to be a dad and take care of her. I was a hands-on dad and never said no to any request related to her. My life script led me to always want to be a family man and I had a strong desire to be a father. When this moment arrived, I was totally in love with it. This is a telltale sign that the Ego has you. I fell hopelessly in love with something outside of me. Something which always changes, and I relied on that love to make me happy. This is the Ego trick. When you rely on something outside of you for love you are stating that you must believe you have a lack inside of you that needs filling; then the Ego has you under its control. Thankfully I had given my Ego and this relationship to Guru-Je so it was him managing this, and Jesus says in the course, "I inspire all miracles," so it was in his hands. I remember when my mum came to visit the baby when she was born and while holding her she spoke and implied that she knew much more about taking care of my child than me and tried to take over the caring. Of course this was my interpretation which is my perception, and it came as a huge wave of attack from the Ego. I was boiling inside and about to either defend or attack back through words but I went into the now presence, I was silent and I grinded out the forgiveness inside because I knew my mum was a projection of the mind, my body wasn't really there and this whole episode was a scene created as an opportunity to release the pain I had from the separation from God. Because this was very hard for me to handle it took me to my limits. Describing this metaphorically it was as if I had to leave the stage and become an audience member sitting next to Guru-Je watching this dream figure Akash on stage with his mum and baby. It was as if I was not there as I stepped back and out of the play. *In this Sp-Ace illusions cannot touch you, you have the Ace to win the hand, you have the hand of God holding you up.* Behaviorally I was silent also. I smiled, said to my mum that she must be an expert to have had us three children and I left the room for fresh air. I was defenseless and I trusted my Guru. Guru-Je held me up just as I felt I was about to fall. The Holy Spirit will never let you down, its love is limitless, and its strength is of God.

You're really only forgiving yourself:
With forgiveness you always need to remember that you aren't forgiving the other person for what they appear to do; it's a mirror image of yourself, the situation is telling you what's in your mind. An outward projection of an inward condition. The more forgiveness you do, the more Love, Joy and peace you encounter in every situation. As the darkness in the mind evaporates the light fills it with the vastness of what you are. Another way to look at this is the person is acting the way you reacted to God. The figure is just an actor playing it out for you. If you look close enough you will realize that moment cannot be brought back again. The feelings and intensity are left there, the scene slowly fades away back into consciousness and it's not real because you cannot touch it, feel it or be there again. It was made only for you to forgive. If you don't forgive another scene will pop up with apparently different characters and a different set, the one who's awake, sees right through it, surrenders into the present moment and forgives accordingly. Guru-Je will then adjust space-time or shorten it so another lesson is not needed. Not one stone will remain unturned as Jesus walks through each stone that contains unconscious

Guilt. You will be restored back to your real state of mind the way God created you.

It's an attitude until it just happens automatically, and you master it:

At the very start of forgiveness, it was as if I had my whole hand gripped onto my Ego very tightly, and like a child who has firm grip of their toy rattle and doesn't want to let it go I was extremely frightened to death to let Guruji or Jesus have it. Actually, looking back now, I wasn't frightened to death, the Ego was frightened to death, because it knows it's all made up and can only exist if I believe in it. Death isn't real, it's the extinguishing of the Ego. The real you is immortal. So at the start it's like Guru-Je is saying just loosen your fingertip ever so much, I'm here, nothing will happen to you, I will help you if you just let me. You can't yet heal yourself, but you can allow yourself to be healed by the Holy Spirit. Like a bird with an injured wing doesn't want anyone to touch it, the Guru gently heals you so you can fly to freedom. This really can only happen if you completely trust the Holy Spirit and God your creator. This relationship builds up over time. Remember you're not just forgiving 24 hours a day, seven days a week. The Guru knows what you like in the world after all you've handed over your Ego to it. The Holy Spirit sprinkles little breadcrumbs of the things you are attracted to so you can keep motivated, carry on with the undoing and keep dismantling the make-believe self-image. The amount of times I have been baked cakes from friends is much more than luck, or a family member has sent me over dinner which was a craving I felt, or since I'm a gardener I am given flower bulbs annually to pot in my garden and watch grow into wonderful flowers in the summer. Also since I like my sleep so much – *to rest in God* – he gave me a system where my baby is sleeping from about 7pm to 7am in her own room every day from five months old. The Holy Spirit gives you everything you need and more. Enough money, tools, time alone, physical support from friends and family, trips to nice places, fashionable clothes so you don't look out of place amongst other parents, and any means that makes you comfortable to fulfil your role and forgive what you perceive.

Just to make clear, this is not sacrifice which is willingly losing something to gain something else. Sacrifice is totally alien to God, for He only provides without cost and knows no loss. The Holy Spirit is not asking us to sacrifice all that we hold dear, particularly the things of the body. This lie makes the objective seem fearful. It is the Ego, not God, that demands sacrifice. All of its pleasures come with pain. In fact pain and pleasure are the same thing as they are here to make the body real to us. It asks us to sacrifice wholeness to keep a little treasure for ourselves, yet this "treasure" is only loss, isolation, and fear. The Ego is therefore asking for complete, not part, sacrifice. The real meaning of sacrifice and deprivation, then, is "the cost of believing in illusions". Guru-Je asks only for you to give up the belief in a made-up world. We must give Him not sacrifice, but the whole concept of sacrifice.

Forgiveness is a lifelong commitment. You get to a stage where you are completely unafraid of anything, you know there is no death although the body will end. You understand that life is simply a romantic relationship with yourself, and you enjoy what life brings with a firm guarantee that this path eventually leads to you waking up inside of God, either in this lifetime or another. Jesus says, "Miracles are expressions of love, but they may not always have observable effects." In my experience I would say I have felt the effects on many occasions. All of my fears of possible future situations were made to literally be nothing, untrue and lies, as Guru-Je brings unified perception into your reality. With work, before you give your thoughts away to the Holy Spirit, there's the fear of losing your knowledge without these thoughts, then your credibility, and this becomes a poor performer and eventually being unliked and dismissed. From this comes the fear of not being able to pay your bills, support your family, and believe it or not leading to homelessness and eventually death. This may seem far-fetched but the Ego keeps the death part far enough from you so you keep chasing the world for survival but also keeps the thought of death close enough, so you live in fear. If you hand it over to the Holy Spirit I assure you your life will be more than alright, it will be a happy dream and miraculous things will happen. Guru-Je doesn't give you more possessions, relationships, false power or material items. He changes your perception to look at everything with real sight so in fact you do not need these things for happiness, but just to fulfil its short-lived purpose. For example before I connected I had to drive a new BMW, I had to wear designer clothes, sunglasses and shoes, I had to eat at Michelin star restaurants on a special occasion, and I had to work long hard hours at work in order to feel I did an honest day's work and deserved my position. I had to have a large circle of friends who I socialized with frequently and I was considered popular. When I joined with the Holy Spirit all of these meaningless virtues were dismantled to become what they really are: expressions of lack in myself. I still have my BMW but it's 15 years old, and I see cars as fulfilling their purpose not filling what is appearing to be absent. I never really think about fashion; it's been handed off to the Holy Spirit, and actually to my surprise designer clothes tend to get gifted to me if needed. I hardly buy them myself anymore, as I prefer comfort over flair. There's nothing wrong with being fashionable, but if you get raspberry juice over your white Gucci shirt or over your plain unbranded shirt, what would be more painful to you? It's the one you have identified more with and you're much more likely to be identified with the Gucci since you worked so hard to buy it and you value it as a mental idea. The best thing to do is make everything the same by not making it special. Remembering that *Fav-__our__-ites are here to exclude us from the rest of __ourself.__* This nullifies the pain, but pain sometimes is okay as it brings a forgiveness opportunity. Suddenly this carefree nature takes over and you don't care what people think of you as they are only there as mental thoughts. I lost interest in Michelin star restaurants as food becomes something to fill my stomach with although cravings do appear often as my character enjoys food, but the Holy Spirit manages it perfectly. Sometimes I'm gifted my thoughts (he puts them there to be gifted) and sometimes I'm tested to be happy with what I have. With work I stick to my working hours at the office and don't burn myself out for anyone. That said if Guruji sends me in to help colleagues because I may have the unique skills to complete that task then I'm happy to fulfil my duties. Friends do come and go. Having children has brought me new ones which brings in Ego dynamics like competition, comparisons, and specialness, but when you see through Christ vision you see each child the same, as a mirror image of you, so you don't identify with separation but instead with bringing together and convergence through union.

My Method back to Peace "Going in with Guru-Je" (Guruji Jesus)

I asked Guru-Je how I can explain the way he guides me inwards to the peace, and how this gets me eventually to home. He's asked me to describe how I complete forgiveness through five stages, and then I was guided to three more stages that the Holy Spirit performs for us. Forgiveness is very simple, but hard to do at the start because we need to be trained to go inwards right to the decision-making mind which is hidden by the Ego. The message that comes with this is that anything which has levels is an illusion, because our true state is changeless and constant extending out into eternity, however, since we are here in a dream illusion it's useful to show the movement back to total peace. Let me try to describe to you the mind travel of *"Going in with Guru-Je" (Guruji Jesus)* which is a term we have completely made up ourselves.

5 Stages to my Miracles

Stage 1 – Feeling – You're living your life normally, and suddenly you meet someone and feel anger, fear, and some suffering. Remember not to associate with these feelings, they are not you. Go deeper, know you have a perceptual problem to be corrected as you are interpreting this situation incorrectly.

Stage 2 – Visualize – The people who have caused this problem are the first point to blame; the Ego wants you to attack/condemn them back as they have rattled your Ego's cage. Visualize these people in your mind as bodies as the reference point to start forgiveness.

Stage 3 – Remove the Form – Now remove your visualization in order to go deeper, but you may bring it back for Stage 5 to pinpoint who you are forgiving. If you think they are the people you know, and that they are the ones who have done this to you then you will be met with extreme resistance to wholeheartedly forgive. They are not the cause of your suffering. Remember they are not their bodies either. They are not what you think of them, they are the bringer of the gift. Go deeper inwards.

Stage 4 – My Mind – Removing form is essential but the wave of attack can still feel very threatening. Go deeper to realize they are showing you what's in your mind. It's your unconscious guilt because it's you that believes you have separated from God, and they are innocent and are just showing you the effect of your decision. In some respects, don't shoot the messenger. You haven't really separated from God, that's impossible; you just believe that you have. You are forgiving yourself for what you have not done.

Stage 5 – You are the Decision Maker – This will now close off your pain as you realize this is coming from you, not happening to you; also realizing there is something you can do about this and hand it over to the Holy Spirit. The secret dream is that I tried to destroy God, to be my own God and I believed I authored myself. I chose the wrong teacher and I'm going to choose again now the right teacher by forgiveness. I now bring the visualization from Stage 2 into my mind, but it's not painful anymore as I see the situation for what it really is and say something like:

You're innocent Whole and Spirit. I'm innocent Whole and spirit. All is forgiven, and all is released; the separation from Father never occurred and we're both in perfect oneness with God eternally. I chose the Wrong teacher. I now choose the right teacher. I choose Jesus/Guruji/the Holy Spirit.

Guru-Je will adjust space-time, so you no longer need to go through that in another form, time then shrinks and you're one step closer to home. Peace, Love and Joy will take over from the fear, anger and suffering you felt at Stage 1. I also like to walk off of the "stage of life" and sit in the audience with Guru-Je. In this way I'm completely unattached to the body figure Akash and the other person, so forgiveness is so smooth as I just watch them going through the motions with the master beside me.

The next 3 stages describe the aftereffects of continually forgiving in your life. In Stage 6, all of your lifetime forgiveness prepares for an open mind to receive Grace. Stage 7 is the receiving of Grace. Stage 8 is awakening back inside of God in oneness.

Stage 6 – *"We prepare for grace in that an open mind can hear the* call to awaken. It is not shut tight against God's voice. It has become aware that there are things it does not know, and thus is ready to accept a state completely different from experience with which it is familiarly at home." (W-P1.169.3:2)

Stage 7 – "Grace is an aspect of the Love of God which is most like the state prevailing in the unity of truth. It is the world's most lofty aspiration, for it leads beyond the world entirely. It is past learning, yet the goal of learning, for grace cannot come until the mind prepares itself for true acceptance. Grace becomes inevitable instantly in those who have prepared a table where it can be gently laid and willingly received; an altar clean and holy for the gift." (W-P1.169.1:1)

Stage 8 – "Oneness is simply the idea God is. And in His Being, He encompasses all things. No mind holds anything but Him. We say, 'God is,' and then we cease to speak, for in that knowledge words are meaningless. There are no lips to speak them, and no part of mind sufficiently distinct to feel that it is now aware of something not itself. It has united with its Source. And like its Source Itself, it merely is.

We cannot speak nor write nor even think of this at all. It comes to every mind when total recognition that its will is God's has been completely given and received completely. It returns the mind into the endless present, where the past and future cannot be conceived. It lies beyond salvation; past all thought of time, forgiveness and the holy face of Christ. The Son of God has merely disappeared into his Father, as his Father has in him. The world has never been at all. Eternity remains a constant state."(W-P1.169.5:1)

Communicating with the Holy Spirit

At the beginning of this journey it's rare to be able to communicate directly through conversation with the Holy Spirit because our filter is likely to be distorted by our conditioned mind leading to what was a pure message sent to be overlaid with the unclean Ego Thought system. There are some teachers who claim to have done this and have written books on this and the material speaks for itself. Helen Schucman who channelled *A Course in Miracles* from Jesus is one such example. Clearly the material is not of this world and you couldn't make it up if you tried. It's not that she was Egoless, but that she was chosen to do this in her life script so was given the gift as a messenger to the rest of us.

The main ways the Holy Spirit communicates with you is through pictures, images, feelings, and sensations that are specific to you and which you have a unique interpretation of. It also communicates with me through other people's spoken words which appear to be a different conversation to them but a method of guidance for me directly. I remember when my wife and I learnt the news that we were expecting our second child. She sent me out immediately to go and collect multivitamins for pregnant women, but she doesn't take tablets well so they had to be the liquid sort. I went to the supermarket and glanced over the aisles. I looked repeatedly, and they had all the vitamins except the liquid kind. I stood still, I closed my mind off and I let the Holy Spirit take over fully. I kid you not, this couple joined me at the very end of the aisle, and they were having a conversation. They said, "We have to go to Superdrug today before it closes so hurry up." I saw that as communication, so I left the store but wanted to go to Boots which is my much-preferred store to Superdrug as growing up that was local to me. On my walk to Superdrug to my surprise I walked past a huge queue (line) at Boots and was greeted with no queue at all at Superdrug. I was guided to go to the far end of the store and there it was. "Buy 2 get the 3rd free" was the deal and the cashier tills had no queue. It was the easiest thing I had ever done. I was so amazed as I passed the Boots queue outside. It hadn't moved and I knew I was taken care of.

As I moved through the course Jesus communicated with me with lines of the course. As a situation arose in my life words would enter my mind and the interpretation given instantly so

I wouldn't miss it. I remember when I was meeting an uncle of mine who had recently been having cancer treatment and we were invited to his house. This uncle knew me before I was married to my wife so knew me in my Egoic days. I was nervous to meet him. The words that arrived into my mind before the catchup were "true empathy", so I looked it up in the course to refresh my memory, and when I met him I followed it directly. I didn't join in with his suffering, and I didn't follow my Ego and try to heal him either, I let the Holy Spirit take over and actually this was the last time I saw him as he passed away a few months after. I remember in that experience how the relationship was blessed by Guru-Je. My uncle spoke to me like my dad did, I reached out to hold his hand and I never let go of it. It was my physical expression of love to connect to him. As the night ran through its course I could feel an unusual reminder of losing my dad, but this time I was not happy or sad, I was complete, full of strength and confidence that my uncle will be taken care of by our creator and grateful for all the experiences we shared together. *A Course in Miracles* says:

True Empathy

To empathize does not mean to join in suffering, for that is what you must refuse to understand. That is the ego's interpretation of empathy, and is always used to form a special relationship in which the suffering is shared. The capacity to empathize is very useful to the Holy Spirit, provided you let Him use it in His way. He does not understand suffering, and would have you teach it is not understandable. When He relates through you, He does not relate through your ego to another ego. He does not join in pain, understanding that healing pain is not accomplished by delusional attempts to enter into it, and lighten it by sharing the delusion.

The clearest proof that empathy as the ego uses it is destructive lies in the fact that it is applied only to certain types of problems and in certain people. These it selects out, and joins with. And it never joins except to strengthen itself. Make no mistake about this maneuver; the ego always empathizes to weaken, and to weaken is always to attack. You do not know what empathizing means. Yet of this you may be sure; if you will merely sit quietly by and let the Holy Spirit relate through you, you will empathize with strength, and will gain in strength and not in weakness.

Your part is only to remember this; you do not want anything you value to come of a relationship. You choose neither to hurt it nor to heal it in your own way. You do not know what healing is. All you have learned of empathy is from the past. And there is nothing from the past that you would share, for there is nothing from the past that you would keep. Do not use empathy to make the past real, and so perpetuate it. Step gently aside, and let healing be done for you. Keep but one thought in mind and do not lose sight of it, however tempted you may be to judge any situation, and to determine your response by judging it. Focus your mind only on this:

I am not alone, and I would not intrude the past upon my Guest.
I have invited Him, and He is here.
I need do nothing except not to interfere.

True empathy is of Him Who knows what it is. You will learn His interpretation of it if you let Him use your capacity for strength, and not for weakness. He will not desert you, but be sure that you desert not Him. Humility is strength in this sense only; that to recognize and accept the fact that you do not know is to recognize and accept the fact that He does know. You are not sure that He will do His part, because you have never yet done yours completely. You cannot know how to respond to what you do not understand. Be tempted not in this, and yield not to the ego's triumphant use of empathy for its glory. (T-16.I.1:1)

The Holy Spirit also communicates with you in your dreams. I have had many moments when the words of *A Course in Miracles* are recited to me while I lay down to sleep, situations in my day are run over in my mind and Guru-Je is going through it with me with the course's material. It's like he's fine-combing the lesson and drilling it into me, so I forgive it clearly before I deep sleep. Sometimes this can take an hour or two, and I'm in a lot of peace although the Ego meets with resistance and makes up trivial reasons to ignore the communication and go to sleep. Reasons like if I don't sleep the next day it will apparently be difficult taking care of the baby as I'll be tired. Tiredness is only a mental belief and is part of our conditioning. You can't be tired when with the Holy Spirit as _it is_ your go-to place for rest. When you sleep where do you think you are going except to the peace and quiet to rejuvenate from the World of the Ego? If you can't sleep due to worry and stress then you have identified with the Ego and it doesn't want you to rest; it has a grip on you.

I truly enjoy the way the Holy Spirit connects with me through music. It is so loving and gives a unique message just for me. The way it does this is when the songs are played, the words are given a distinctive meaning as the song is played back into my mind. The interpretations can be a loving message, a hello or guidance in some way. When I was halfway through my course studies I remember Guru-Je was working with me and undoing the Ego. He was bringing up emotions I have hidden deep inside so I can forgive them and hand them over to him. Lots of my unconscious guilt came to the surface as I began to see all the lies which I had believed. I had believed I was really separate from my creator, alone and independent, ruler of my own world and able to do what I wish. Guilt came through immensely because despite all of this, I was loved unconditionally by God, and that love was unbreakable. That love was so much that I remember being speechless in trying to describe it and then I said in my mind, "Why would I have ever wanted to come to this world when with you I am this forever shining white light that covers everything with no interruption or limit anywhere, where everything is unified in flawless unity, where it's impossible to envisage anything outside because there is no place where this light is not?" The answer came to me as, "Let Her Go." I searched for it on the web and there it was, a song by Passenger. I replaced "Her" with "God" and my interpretation was I came here for duality, to be an "I", a "self-personality", and I let God go to experience highs/lows, hot/cold, love/hatred and ups and downs. As the song played I stood there stunned at the way the answer arrived to me. As he sung, the words cut through me as it focused how in my past I constantly chose my Egoic self over and over. I wanted to make my dream go on and on, but no matter how much I wanted it, it will always just be a dream. I could see my Egoic life and the song showing me everything that I experienced was sure to end and the song described very well what life without God is like and that this world was designed to block that love. My question was answered through an everyday worldly popular song.

I also remember another time, which was the day before I had to present figures to the executive board for my job. The Ego was trying to provoke me to identify with it as I could feel deep anxiety and worry attempting to rise. Fear of failure which is not really failure – it's a form of death unnatural to the child of God – wanted to consume me. I immediately forgave it and an hour or so after I took my little toddler for some soft play fun. While she was enjoying the trampoline Wake Me Up by Avicii played on the radio. This was a "Hi, I'm here and I love you" message as the words covered me with Love, confidence and strength. The next day I presented the information and it really helped the board with insights as my higher self flowed through.

My toddler loves to watch *The Lion King*. When I was sitting with her my mind was going through the storyline and the Holy Spirit was showing me the deeper meaning hidden by the Ego. The child believing the lies of his wicked uncle, that he killed his father, destroyed the pride and his home and needs to run away and never come back. Then tries to make a life for himself with a warthog and meerkat but that wasn't real life as it wasn't his natural environment; it wasn't his home. Then being called back home by his beloved childhood friend and having to face the fear, only to find that his only mistake was to believe his uncle's lies. Once this fear was overcome, he returned back to his home and took his rightful place in the kingdom. It's very sneaky of the Ego to put something so close to the truth into a child's cartoon so we would never think there was any truth in it! The message is right under our nose.

The Holy Spirit is always with us, always reminding us of what we are, how much we are loved, how beautiful we really are and how there is nothing to fear at all. The next chapter on Guruji describes his essence which I chose to connect with. This essence is the Holy Spirit or universal mind.

Chapter Five

Guruji

*– **The Guru** is the symbol we use that connects us to our Higher Self, which is Omnipresent. Om-ni-present is where the Holy "**Om**" (the sound of the universe) brings us into the Divine's **Presence**. –*

The Gurus for you

When I first heard that there was a Guru called Guruji who helps people with all of their problems, cures them of diseases and takes care of people's lives, I was very suspicious. Being suspicious is essential, because that vigilant, inquiring mind within you trying to separate truth from illusions gets us back home. Like myself, we all must go through this process ourselves to conclude whether a person is genuine or not. I have heard of and met many so-called masters who claimed to lead me to God if I would submit and let them become my master. The course calls a false idol any "God" that we worship and look to for salvation. Its purpose is to do for us that which we cannot do for ourselves for we believe it possesses the power and magic that we lack as a substitute for God. In essence these idols are ideas which we have placed our faith in for our safety and our happiness. They come as power, fame, money, physical pleasure; idols can be pills, influence, clothing, prestige, being liked, knowing the "right" people and an endless list of forms of nothingness that you endow with magical powers. Basically, an idol is anything outside of us that we hope to make us complete.

Guruji is inside of us. Like Jesus and Buddha, he wants nothing from you except to let him take away your belief that you are little and replace it with what you really are. He's selfless because he is in his perfect state of being as God created him and doesn't need anything from you. His love for you is uninterrupted. It flows like an eternal fountain which was always there and always will be. He gives to you what your inheritance is, unlimited eternal bliss. He walks within you as you walk through all of the dark corners of your mind. He shines our light on everything which we fear and shows us it's nothing at all. Like when we open the curtains in a dark room the darkness just evaporates as the light replaces it, this is what he does to our apparent problems. When you connect to him, you connect to God's presence. The course is very clear though. Jesus is our respected elder brother and is our equal, and "awe" should be kept only for our creator God. This is the same for Guruji, who is our equal beloved elder brother that we are so grateful and indebted to. God on the other hand is the one who created us, and this is an indescribable level of magnificence.

The history here on earth about Guruji is he is the Avatar of Lord Shiva. Lord Shiva is the supreme self who manifested here to show us the way back Home, and Guruji is Shiva, who has come because some part of you has called him for assistance. Guruji was the divine light born on 7th July 1954, in a farming village called Dugri in Punjab, India. His parents realized that their son was no ordinary person very early in his life. He was a Mahapurusha (Supreme Spirit), which means he had already merged with the Divine. When people asked of his name, he would say that the personality of such a one as him had no name because there was no self-identity left. The purpose of his body was to deliver humanity from its sufferings. People flooded to Guruji for deliverance from problems mostly material, of home, jobs, businesses and diseases. His powers spread across the whole of Punjab as people sought him out. This then grew to Jalandhar, Chandigarh, Panchkula and New Delhi where people came from other parts of India and all over the World to seek his blessings. The tea and the blessed food served at Guruji's satsangs (spiritual sacred gatherings) were endowed with special divine blessings. There was always one rule: you must eat and drink all of the food and tea with not a single bit left. This was because he had blessed the food to heal the devotees and there are countless incidents when devotees were healed by just partaking in it. If there was a chili in your plate it was a test of faith. His doors were open to everyone; his message was that there was one God and one universal brotherhood of humanity. To him and for his disciples (the Sangat), the votary of his worshipers were supreme. In return all he wanted was his devotees to become good human beings, to criticize no one, to help everybody they can and to harm no one. He explains that his blessings are not just for this life alone but extended to self-realization. He never delivered any sermons. His was a process of practical spirituality, and he often announced his teachings via the shabads (hymns or sacred songs) that captured the hearts of those who sat around him. This was so his message was received by the devotee in ways that were public as well as intimate due to the sacred connection between the Guru and the disciple. This connection was the very root of the relationship. It lifted the devotee's life to a level where Joy, fulfilment and peace came easy. The shabads became a beacon that always showed the disciple his true aim. When Guruji left his form on 31st May 2007, it was in a way a lesson. He had told his devotees time after time of how momentary life was. He has a temple for his devotees called Bade Mandir and there are a couple of mementos he always leaves for his disciples to show his presence. Firstly an "OM" sign and secondly a smell of roses. I connected with him after he left his form. At the start I always thought my Guru would be here in the physical but actually it worked out perfectly for me that this was not to be.

You will know who your Guru is when you connect to them. I felt rescued, saved from danger, my heart melted as he knew everything about me and still loved me unconditionally with zero judgment. This love is not from this world. Let me share some experiences of meeting Gurus that I interpreted as not genuine below.

The Gurus that are Not for you /
Great teachers in the world

Shortly after my dad passing, I was quite vulnerable and I visited a Hindu Temple with my wife to try to find a spiritual way forward. I had some personal conversations with a few of the members who live there and found out that there was a hierarchy similar to the organizations I have worked in which there are the junior members who tend to be younger put up front to promote Hinduism and perform at festivals to attract new recruits into the circuit; then there were more senior long-term committed members who were very knowledgeable of Hindu scriptures and classified themselves as masters. Above them were the senior leaders that were more political and were revered like Gods. At first I loved their faith in God and it was a huge attraction for me, but as I looked closer and closer I couldn't find God. All I could see were layers of rituals, modern Indian culture in the UK and organization makeup where in order to find liberation you had to work up the ladder to become a master Guru and then a respected leader. My wife could sense this early and we discussed the strangeness of it all. After work one day before I had ever started *A Course in Miracles,* I felt the need to swing by the temple and give some fresh fruit to the deities. I was talking to a young new member and suddenly he says, "Meet my master." I turned around and he stared at me. He was wearing the traditional priestly clothes and he spoke fast to me. He said, "Do you work?" I said, "Yes, I work and I've come with some fruit to offer the deities." He said, "That's good but can I recommend you offer a donation for the temple bus to me now? We need petrol so we can reach a holy conference tomorrow." I stood there stunned. I felt like this person had a nerve to ask me so directly and never even introduced himself as courtesy. I was a little heartbroken because I was hoping this path would be the one for me but I definitely had the feeling that I'm being used and this boy was under the influence of this man that controls him. I gave him £10 as a donation to the universe, gave the fruit and left never to return. Since this was way before *A Course in Miracles*, I never had a chance to forgive until now. Always remember to always go with your inner self who will relay the truth to you for guidance. Looking back now I can see the Holy Spirit was showing me that I was looking in the wrong place, I was looking outward in the Ego world for God, and that master was leading me to the Guru for me. He was telling me to go inward. When I got home, I sincerely prayed to God to help me to find the truth about life, existence, and self-realization. This was shortly before I was introduced to Guruji.

As a born Hindu our religion has so many people who claim to be Gurus and it's a very complicated area to navigate through and find the right one as we are mostly always looking only to the outside. Some tell you to stand on a table in a Yoga position and strip your clothes off to apparently discipline you. Some tell you to do things for them directly or their cause and it can feel like a cult. Some are completely filled with rituals to apparently give you "shakti" or divine power, and others give you materials which are so hard to follow that when you ask the teacher questions you receive answers which can leave you even more confused than before the question was asked. The truth is it has already been decided who the teachers and students are, based on what is best for them in a view of their level of understanding. Pupils have been waiting for the teacher. It is only a matter of time that they come forth into our experience.

We should remember there are some great spiritual teachers out there still, Eckhart Tolle, Mooji, David Hoffmeister, Gary Renard & Deepak Chopra, who can help to guide you to the truth; however, your inner guide is like the fingerprint of God and is your internal voice.

More on A Course in Miracles

A Course in Miracles is a pure non-dualistic pathway; that means it follows the truth that there is only one reality that is real, God's reality. The other reality doesn't exist, only as a dream. No other pathway worked for me as Jesus explains that my way will be different in *A Course in Miracles*. The difference between others and ACIM is others focus on silencing the mind, contemplation, and deep meditation. Sometimes meditating eight to fifteen hours a day. In *A Course in Miracles* Jesus says a Holy relationship is given as means of saving time. He even calls some of the traditional methods tedious and time consuming where we can save thousands of years for you and everyone else. His workbook is designed to be used in any conceivable environment and situation you can think of. The other vital difference is the course gives clear continuous guidance throughout and you don't need a physical Guru to assist you.

Guidance is the Holy Spirit's use of what the Ego made. The Egoic system made the words and the judgments. When the mind descended from a very united loving state to a very chaotic state the Ego created judgment to bring and sustain order into chaos. Like nursery school teachers bring order by rules to toddlers regarding mess and play, it needs order to minimize the need for complete chaos. However, at the same time it needs the chaos to drive fear so doesn't want you to give it up. All defense mechanisms are there to minimize and keep fear, that's why we have to lay down all of our defenses and surrender to the guidance.

The course is a complete self-study spiritual thought system. As a three-volume curriculum consisting of a Text, Workbook for Students and a Manual for Teachers it teaches the remembering of God by undoing guilt through forgiving others. Although the language of the course is that of traditional Christianity it expresses a nonsectarian, nondenominational spirituality. *A Course in Miracles* is therefore a universal spiritual teaching, not a religion. With this course you do not need to find a Guru. Jesus is the Guru, however, if you are more comfortable with another symbol of a Guru this also works. For me it was Guruji with Jesus interchangeably. They link me to my inner voice and I hear it clearly. Jesus isn't interested in 70-90% commitment to this course, he doesn't want you to do a few miracles here and there and then say work got to me and financial issues came so I had to deal with that. It's a lifelong commitment. He says this course will be believed entirely or not at all. Don't put first your career, kids, family, body, health, home, worldly causes, and social life. Flip it and make God your priority. I don't mean this in an ignorant way where you say God will put the food into my baby's mouth so I can quit my job now. That's insane. I mean the trust that the money, the food, the shelter, the clothing along with peace and joy will arrive as we focus on God. If you water a few leaves in the tree they will blossom, but if you water the entire tree the tree takes care of your little area of leaves and the rest. Build your connection with that which takes care of all of itself and the parts you have responsibility for will be taken care of accordingly.

The "Christ" takes many forms. These Masters are the manifestation of the Holy Spirit. *A Course in Miracles* uses Jesus. Use the one which makes you most comfortable to connect with as the Non-Ego Part of you. Examples of some are here:

GURUJI   JESUS of the CHRIST

GURU NANAK   BUDDHA   KRISHNA

Chapter Six

The Body

*– In our World **Anyone** is **Anybody**. If we discard the "**Any**" we correctly have what is true, the **Universal One Body**. –*

The Body as a Projection

We discussed earlier that the Body is a Projection of the Mind, and that actually they are the same entity. In the secret dream Jesus basically tells us that there is no Gap between them. It may appear that the body starts in the world and ends in the world, and that all else before the start and after the end is questionable. This is an illusion. A projection has no reality to it independently from its source. When I'm putting my baby to sleep and I have a small projector showing a moving picture on the ceiling with music playing *Twinkle, Twinkle Little Star*, I don't actually believe the projected images are really independent from the slide. It's showing you what's on the slide reel by shining a light through a transparent lens onto the ceiling. Similarly, the mind is projecting out your body and all the other objects and scenes. Remember the split mind is consciousness. The body and all we see here is a part of the one consciousness. Like the reel of images and the projected activity on the ceiling are the same, the mind and the body are the same. Let's take this further.

So in a projector we have a reel of images that circulate, and when an image reaches the lens at the front, the light shines the image onto the ceiling. The images on the reel after and before they reach and go past the lens are always there despite no longer appearing on the ceiling as projected activity. It's the reel of images that is the source of the images on the ceiling. They are the same. This is similar to the body-mind. The split mind is dreaming many thoughts, desires, images, not on a circular reel like a projector; but it does have a circular nature to it as it recreates new bodies, new situations and new pictures to represent its desires and thoughts. These desires and thoughts are projected outwards for a certain interval of time into a world with scenes and bodies. Like the projector, where the images before they arrive at the lens and after they leave the lens are always present despite no longer appearing on the ceiling – the dream is still happening in the mind before the body's birth and after the body dissolves. It's all a dream. The illusion is that we live and die here. When we complicate this further with past lives, future lives, all scenarios of situations occurring all at once through the space-time continuum, we can see just how grand and magnificent this design really is. Our mind is incredible. We can't dismiss the entire design as just an illusion; it's a factory house full of information. Yes it's a dream but is far from trivial.

We need to remember that the split mind is projecting this dream and is made up of two opposing thought systems, The Ego & The Holy Spirit. The body and its environment appear to suffer through the Ego's picture projection, but really the pain is in the mind because we have chosen the Ego as our teacher. To go further, it suffers because it's a dream without its creator. If we choose the Holy Spirit through Jesus, Guruji, Buddha etc. we are healing our mind and the moving pictures around you (including the body) – the world will show you this as your experience.

Jesus on The Body

Let's see what Jesus in *A Course in Miracles* says about the Body with my interpretation of it below each paragraph.

What is the Body
The body is a fence the Son of God imagines he has built, to separate parts of his Self from other parts. It is within this fence he thinks

he lives, to die as it decays and crumbles. For within this fence he thinks that he is safe from love. Identifying with his safety, he regards himself as what his safety is. How else could he be certain he remains within the body, keeping love outside? (W-PII.5.1:1)

The first two sentences are very clear. We are **imagining** ourselves to be separate from each other, and **we** have built this separation. It's not done to us, it's our alignment to the Ego which has projected out this fragmented appearance. The third sentence – how we think we are safe from love – should cut through our delusions. Outside of this imagined self sits total complete love which we do not want. We then identify with this false safety to ensure we stay as a body repeatedly, i.e. we keep the separated mind active by protecting this imagined self and we then project new bodies and live apparent "lives" over and over.

The body will not stay. Yet this he sees as double safety. For the Son of God's impermanence is "proof" his fences work, and do the task his mind assigns to them. For if his oneness still remained untouched, who could attack and who could be attacked? Who could be victor? Who could be his prey? Who could be victim? Who the murderer? And if he did not die, what "proof" is there that God's eternal Son can be destroyed? (W-PII.5.1:2)

This self which we have named, mine is Akash, has completely identified with the body. It thinks it is the body. Yet the body will die and this makes a double safety for Akash the "person":

(1) If we make it a fact that the body can die then we prove the separate part is separate from the whole.
(2) If the body can die then that's proof that the Child of God (the whole true self) can die.

By believing our oneness can be distorted we can believe in

victims and villains, and that our bodies can be attacked or defended. Obviously this is delusional, and represents the delusional thought system we have affiliated with in the Ego.

The body is a dream. Like other dreams it sometimes seems to picture happiness, but can quite suddenly revert to fear, where every dream is born. For only love creates in truth, and truth can never fear. Made to be fearful, must the body serve the purpose given it. But we can change the purpose that the body will obey by changing what we think that it is for. (W-PII.5.1:3)

The body is always changing, but the inner being is changeless. When something is always changing how can it have any reality? The body is a dream. In a dream there seems to be pleasure and pain but in Truth there is only unlimited Joy in Love. The body is what you desire it to be. If you want it to serve the Ego it will be a painful experience, but it can be given to the Holy Spirit to return the mind back to stability.

The body is the means by which God's Son returns to sanity. Though it was made to fence him into hell without escape yet has the goal of Heaven been exchanged for the pursuit of hell. The Son of God extends his hand to reach his brother, and to help him walk along the road with him. Now is the body holy. Now it serves to heal the mind that it was made to kill. (W-PII.5.1:4)

If you change your goal to Heaven instead of trying to be a separate self, on this journey all of the other apparent parts of the self unify with you to make the body holy; then can the body serve to heal the mind that wanted to destroy.

You will identify with what you think will make you safe. Whatever it may be, you will believe that it is one with you. Your safety lies in truth, and not in lies. Love is your safety. Fear does not exist.

Identify with love, and you are safe. Identify with love, and you are home. Identify with love and find your Self. (W-PII.5.1:5)

If you want to be safe then identify with Love which is Truth. If you surrender to fear and listen to its lies you will feel lost.

Remember that the Holy Spirit interprets the body only as a means of communication. Being the Communication Link between God and His separated Sons, the Holy Spirit interprets everything you have made in the light of what He is. The ego separates through the body, the Holy Spirit reaches through it to others. You do not perceive your brothers as the Holy Spirit does, because you do not regard bodies solely as a means of joining minds and uniting them with yours and mine. This interpretation of the body will change your mind entirely about its value. Of itself it has none.
If you use the body for attack, it is harmful to you. If you use it only to reach the minds of those who believe they are bodies, and teach them through the body that this is not so, you will understand the power of the mind that is in you. If you use the body for this and only for this, you cannot use it for attack. In the service of uniting it becomes a beautiful lesson in communion, which has value until communion is. This is God's way of making unlimited what you have limited. The Holy Spirit does not see the body as you do, because he knows the only reality of anything is the service it renders God on behalf of the function he gives it. (T-8.7.2:1)

Growing up all of my life I always thought my body was me. If someone punched me I would feel pain, if someone kissed me I would feel pleasure, if I studied all night for an exam I would feel tired and if I played five-a-side football for two hours I would feel exhausted. Reading the above from Jesus who is the all-knowing Holy Spirit manifested, I clearly didn't understand the disconnection between my real being and the body. When I first read that the body was a communication device, I immediately asked Guruji what on earth that meant. A picture of a phone emerged into my mind, and as I further interrogated the master it was slowly emerging that the body was in fact nothing but a dream figure. It's constantly changing. Like a moving picture it continuously shifts in age, gains wrinkles, it withers and eventually recycles back into the universal dream in dirt or ashes. Its purpose is for only one thing, to communicate with other bodies by letting the Holy Spirit flow through it to other bodies, and the message to them is simple, "You are not this body or person, you are the Child of God." He showed me a phone because it's temporary. We try to dress it with fancy covers, we give it so much importance it becomes a part of us. It's always changing with updates and upgrades and it needs recharging just like the body does at night. The main function of the phone is to communicate with other phones and the message is sent through the phone to the receiver on the other side. However, the phone isn't really that important to us; it's not really a part of me, just like the body I am so much more than it. The next point emerges, why is the body anything to me? What it is made of is not precious. Jesus goes on to tell us:

> just as certainly it has no feeling. It transmits to you the feelings that you want. Like any communication medium the body receives and sends the messages that it is given. It has no feeling for them. All of the feeling with which they are invested is given by the sender and the receiver. The ego and the Holy Spirit both recognize this, and both also recognize that here the sender and receiver are the same. The Holy Spirit tells you this with joy. The ego hides it, for it would keep you unaware of it. Who would send messages of hatred and attack if he but understood he sends them to himself? Who would accuse, make guilty and condemn himself? (T-19.8.6:2)

This explanation takes this conversation to a whole other level. The body doesn't actually feel anything, it feels what the mind tells it to feel. Think about it, why do we all appear to have different pain tolerances, because our conditioned mind has different levels of awareness. If you are a guiltless mind like Christ or Guruji you cannot suffer as you are as innocent as Father who created us. But if you really believe you are this person with this body then you will feel guilty and suffer. The sender of the message and the receiver of the message are the same. I.e. the person who is speaking and the person being spoken to are the same being, but the Ego will want to hide this from us so we don't love the other as ourself.

For the first 30 years of my life I had this all wrong. As I had identified with the Ego I had put the body through so much hardship. The guilt from being separated from God was projected onto my body and it was appearing to be draining my life. The Ego is a master trickster. It firstly promoted drinking alcohol regularly at college, university and in my late 20s, eating such a fussy food diet (to feel special in my choices), and then when I reached a certain age it went the other way. I lost all my weight and was at the gym six days a week sculpting and shaping my body which came with strict diets of high protein and low carbohydrates every day, and I was a slave to the Ego. This was all to keep me occupied with the body, to keep me mindless so I don't go inwards. My neutral body as a communication medium was fatigued on the surface all because I joined with the wrong teacher, the Ego.

As I reflect on this, the Ego even now tries to show me the causation of my suffering was all here in the body. That my choices here are what has made my body ache. This is a lie. The causation was from the mind and the body is a projection of the pain in the mind, created by the separation from God. If I wake up in the morning with backache it's not because of how I slept or what I did yesterday. The root cause of the pain is the guilt within my mind that I have projected onto my body at the moment of separation. It needs to be forgiven and released.

The Body's Health

I asked Guruji how the body needs to be cared and nurtured for, and how to deal with sickness. He guided me to this:

The body's health is fully guaranteed, because it is not limited by time, by weather or fatigue, by food and drink, or any laws you made it serve before. You need do nothing now to make it well, for sickness has become impossible. Yet this protection needs to be preserved by careful watching. If you let your mind harbor attack thoughts, yield to judgment or make plans against uncertainties to come, you have again misplaced yourself, and made a bodily identity which will attack the body, for the mind is sick. Give instant remedy, should this occur, by not allowing your defensiveness to hurt you longer. Do not be confused about what must be healed, but tell yourself:

I have forgotten what I really am, for I mistook my body for myself. Sickness is a defense against the truth. But I am not a body. And my mind cannot attack. So, I cannot be sick. (W-P1.136.18:3)

He also guided me to:

The body is in need of no defense. This cannot be too often emphasized. It will be strong and healthy if the mind does not abuse it by assigning it to roles it cannot fill, to purposes beyond its scope, and to exalted aims which it cannot accomplish. Such attempts, ridiculous yet deeply cherished, are the sources for the many mad attacks you make upon it. For it seems to fail your hopes, your needs, your values and your dreams.

The "self" that needs protection is not real. The body, valueless and hardly worth the least defense, need merely be perceived as quite apart from you, and it becomes a healthy, serviceable instrument through which the mind can operate until its usefulness is over. Who would want to keep it when its usefulness is done? (W-P1.135.7:1)

Body Symptoms can be a concern, the body suffers like a mask to bury what really suffers underneath. The mind. There's a trick happening, a major distraction is going on to keep the mind from seeing it is the one that suffers. It's not the body that suffers, it's the mind telling the body what to feel and the mind projects symptoms onto the body to make it very believably seem like there is an outside problem to be fixed. The Body is outside of you; you think it's surrounding you but it's outside the mind. Jesus gives us an analogy. Children play with toys in order to be entertained, when they play with toys they are awestruck and are in a world of their own with their figures and they're playing as if they're grown-ups and telling the figurines what to do, what to say, what to feel, and that's what the entertainment is. How fun it is that I can give realism to these dolls, and this is what is happening in the mind. When we talk about sickness and disease the mind allocates disease to the body as if the body has the disease. This is reinforced by the conditioning from our upbringing in life and the medical profession doesn't tell us blood pressure is in the mind, cancer is in the mind, heart disease is in the mind. They give us a couple of categories with lots of forms to focus on and conceal the one problem we believe, and even this isn't a problem as the separation from God hasn't happened in reality. Categories are (1) mental illness and (2) physical sickness. Mental Illness examples are Major Depression, Anxiety Disorders, Phobias, Schizophrenia and Eating/Personality disorders. Physical sickness are diseases of the body like Cancer, Diabetes, Rubella, Alzheimer's, Heart Disease – the Ego attacks everything it perceives by breaking it into small, disconnected parts, without meaningful relationships, and therefore without meaning. You can either believe you are this body who has this disease, or that you are not the body and the dis-ease is of the mind. If you believe the latter, then you would forgive yourself for hiding the causation of the illness in the body, and step back and go deep inwards to watch whatever the body appears to go through. In this place you're in Love and you're taken care of. It's a trick of the Ego for us to believe that there are external diseases causing this suffering. Jesus calls this madness below:

> *Think of the freedom in the recognition that you are not bound by all the strange and twisted laws you have set up to save you. You really think that you would starve unless you have stacks of green paper strips and piles of metal discs. You really think a small round pellet or some fluid pushed into your veins through a sharpened needle will ward off disease and death. You really think you are alone unless another body is with you.*
> *It is insanity that thinks these things. You call them laws, and put them under different names in a long catalogue of rituals that have no use and serve no purpose. You think you must obey the "laws" of medicine, of economics and of health. Protect the body, and you will be saved.*
> *These are not laws, but madness. The body is endangered by the mind that hurts itself. The body suffers just in order that the mind will fail to see it is the victim of itself. The body's suffering is a mask the mind holds up to hide what really suffers. It would not understand it is its own enemy; that it attacks itself and wants to die. It is from this your "laws" would save the body. It is for this you think you are a body. There are no laws except the laws of God.* (W-P1.76.3:1)

Jesus is starting to allow us to remember our spiritual mastery. He's saying when your time comes you won't need injections, medication, tablets to heal you, your mind will be fully healed so illness won't be projected on to the body. That said, most of us are not there yet, so what I do is give it over to Guru-Je to decide for me what to take and when to have it. He is omnipresent, knows all of the future, the past and all possible scenarios of this life to the end of time so why wouldn't you give it over to him?

Because your fear-based little Ego wants to be independent from its source and doesn't want to surrender to Love. This is all about your level of faith, the people here who really believe they are this body will call this selfish or foolish, but they can't see past the little box they are in, they can't see their interconnectedness to everything as they have closed themselves off to be lonely and fearsome. By following only your higher self it will make sure everyone around you has the loving outcome. The real you inside you is Spirit and it has a mind which is the activating agent. The body is a projection of this so it's like if you went to a theatre and watched a play and saw an act of the English plague full of disease and sickness – you wouldn't go up to the characters and call an ambulance for a hospital. They are playing the script. Now your body is part of that script, so if it gets up and calls an ambulance then it's following its lines. The mind is projecting the sickness onto the body. On a deeper metaphysical level, that mind believed that it could leave God. It was so horrific and dark that these dark attack thoughts were pushed out of awareness and then the mind needed a hiding place so it wouldn't feel so guilty, so it projected out a world of physical images which Akash and all of the readers of this book are appearing to be inside of. Then it put the guilt onto the character in different forms. Akash says I have a virus, I have the flu, cancer, heart disease and it's all part of that false cause effect. Yes the body may well have these illnesses, but that wasn't caused here, it's caused from the mind despite everyone who believes they are this body here telling you otherwise. All illness comes from believing in separation from God but that is at such a high level we need intermediate steps to get towards that. Firstly there's tremendous fear of thoughts. We think we separated from God and can think thoughts separate from God which leads to miscreation. God created us pure spirit but we rejected this and wanted to play the game of space-time. The perfect light wasn't enough, and the fact we think we can miscreate and create differently than God is dreadful and frightening (there's a Gap in the mind) also known as the unholy instant. So the trick the Ego does to deal with the horror is it creates a make-believe world and projects to it bodies which are puppets where the mind is the puppeteer.

We are attracted to finding the sources of the sickness in the world. It's like the child who is so entertained with the puppets that it just wants to play with the puppets and not look at the mind. It's easier to try to find the causes of sickness in the world than to forgive especially when the game looks so attractive that it's too much to look into our mind for every scrap of guilt and fear, and hand it over to the light. There's a time when a child has to grow up and let go of its toys. Sickness is not the causation of anything, it's the consequence. The truth cannot be found by investigating those symptoms. We have to go to where the real cause is. Healing comes from atonement, which is undoing the Ego. There's no healing without realizing this world is not real. Realizing this and having this recognition replaces the entire world you see with clearer perception of it. This will give you the power over your mind from anything in the world. You are completely free. We shouldn't focus on the specific symptoms. If you do that you will forget that there is only one problem, the decision to be an "I"; forgive it.

Let's bring this conversation back into the world we live in for practical reasons. All the above is true but people around us are actually getting sick and I wanted to disclose that recently, I was sick. I don't usually get sick but this time I apparently caught a bug from my child at nursery which gave me a few days of clogged-up nose, loss of taste and a repetitive cough. I intellectually knew that the problem wasn't a bug from the nursery as sickness is from the mind, not from body-to-body transfer. So, I searched my mind for grievances which I must have been holding to breed attack thoughts. After much searching, I found what I was looking for. I had a personal issue still with a close member of my family, and I was holding onto it as a personal attack. I knew this was causing the illness and it needed immediate forgiveness. I linked it back to the only problem there actually ever is, the separation from God. I forgave myself for projecting this onto my family member and I forgave them for what they didn't do. I also forgave myself for projecting the pain onto my body as an illness because this was a way to keep the mind grievance hidden and evaluated as a common child bug. Akash being ill was the actor playing the part. It wasn't real because the body was only acting out my grievance in a chosen form, and if you looked closely at it you could see it was showing me what was in my mind when I chose to be separate from God. By detaching from Akash I was not able to suffer at all, the body did not feel at all. In this state there's no feeling of wellness or illness. Following my forgiveness the mind was healed so there was no pain projection onto the body. The mind tells the body how to feel; when it's conflicted about itself and forgotten Christ then it projects pain onto the body as if the body is feeling. Here in the world Akash lost a couple days of his life recovering. The illness here was prescribed as a bacterial infection which I was given antibiotics for. I asked Guru-Je what to do as I was open to take or not take the medication. I fully surrendered and had total trust. On this occasion I was guided to take the medication, but this whole scene was set for me to forgive. It was here as an example to not harbor attack thoughts. The body will go through all kinds of experiences as it ages, but we shouldn't fear this; they are ways of showing us what's in our mind to be forgiven. Anita Kumar's book *The Divine Light* speaks of her cancer treatment and she felt at ease with Guruji by her side. She learnt to disengage her mind from the experience. She went through the motions by detaching herself from the emotions. She calls it her Karma to go through this. In our split mind state we don't have the power to directly cure every issue that we must go through, but we can step away from it and see it outside of us. This is immense freedom. There will be a moment in time when we can directly cure it. As we keep forgiving eventually we will have no Ego whatsoever, where the body becomes elastic and light, Jesus says, *"The guiltless mind cannot suffer and I am as innocent as my father who created me."* (T-5.6.5:1) For now we do have the power to see it for what it is, which is a lie. The course gives you the knowledge to understand what is really going on here and that gives us freedom to change our path. This new direction leads us to a happy dream where eventually it's so peaceful that awakening inside of God is completely natural.

I was recently asked what would happen to me if I was hit by a car. Well, that's a theoretical question. When we go into imagination we go back to the error. When you come back to the present moment the unified mind brings us back into now where I'm not hit by a car, there are no car accidents because the separation from God never occurred. So when we ask the question it's as if in the past there were car accidents and there were different Akash's. Then you ask the question what would happen, see that's a future projection of something that is believed to have occurred, and both of them are distortions to keep the mind at bay from the holy instant of Now. As I follow the guidance from the Holy Spirit and trust it, it's the present moment trust that directs the way. That's not an intellectual thing that's actuality. When you align your mind with the Holy Spirit you align with the state of fearlessness and invulnerability where you are completely safe because you've aligned to spirit and spirit's state is invulnerability and whatever in the world you are perceiving reflects that invulnerability. You don't fear the consequences or that they can come again. If you identify with the body then protection seems like it is a good idea.

As I gave the body over to the Holy Spirit. It ensured it was cared for. In a busy routine with children Guru-Je allowed me to regularly go to the gym, multivitamins were remembered some days and forgotten on others but were taken as required by the one who knows everything, I was given time to mow my lawn and complete my garden for more exercise, and as my wife went deeper into her pregnancy he gave me the energy to step up and take over the physical home affairs.

Once again I wanted to reiterate that the Holy Spirit isn't saying you can share cups of water with your partner who has a contagious virus, it isn't saying to not get life insurance, it isn't saying to wear summer clothes on a winter's cold day or not to put oven gloves on when taking hot food out the oven. Live a normal life and be guided by the spirit on what to do if you are unsure. There's no need to inflate your Ego and think you are more holy than another because you are studying the course. Jesus's mastery was simple, it was mastery of following the Holy Spirit. Living a life like this will eventually lead you to seeing the body as a vehicle outside of you, of which you transmit the holy message of what you are. Always remembering you are the driver of that vehicle; the vehicle isn't driving you. The vehicle needs some maintenance but by leaving that to the expert who knows what the vehicle is, feel assured that you are always safe and secure. Do not feel guilty about illness and don't be afraid of death.

Chapter Seven

Death

*– Every day we all work so mindlessly to meet fear-based **Deadlines**. The bottom **Line** is all fear is fear of being **Dead**, but you can't die as death is a process where only that which is not you ceases to exist. –*

Jesus on Death

We have spoken about the Mind and the Body a lot. The projector analogy makes it very clear that the body doesn't die, the projection just ends and the dream carries on.

Death was one of the main topics I wanted to learn about since my dad left his body. All of the natural questions came to me: Where did he go? Is he united with his parents and loved ones? Does he go to heaven or hell and is there such a thing? What is death, because from the world's view it's a very unhappy experience? Hinduism and most other religions find ways to treat the body with rituals in order to allow the spirit to rest, is this going to make any difference? The course says this about death:

> *There is no death. The Son of God is free. Death is a thought that takes on many forms, often unrecognized. It may appear as sadness, fear, anxiety or doubt; as anger, faithlessness and lack of trust; concern for bodies, envy, and all forms in which the wish to be as you are not may come to tempt you. All such thoughts are but reflections of the worshipping of death as savior and as giver of release.* (W-P1.163.1:1)

This was very new to me. Jesus is saying that death takes on many forms. As we read these forms of death (sadness, fear, anxiety, or doubt, as anger, faithlessness, lack of trust, concern for bodies, envy) we don't see them as death. When we think of death, we think it's people with bodies that lose their life and are not here anymore, but Jesus is saying death forms are the wish to be as you are not and they come to us as temptations to act on it. If we do act on it we are not being what we are. Life is as our true formless being; if we are not "being" ourself then that is not life. Death has no reality, except as a thought, not as an event in the physical world. When the body is relinquished the separated mind which projects the body is still active. Thoughts arise from this mind; if you have lived a life with the Ego as your teacher you will wish for death to finally release the burden of the strains of life. We then associate peace with death and trust in its inevitability. We believe that we are this person, who has lived in this small interval of time and believe that all of the pains and struggles have happened to us; we have chosen to ignore the truth. The truth is the pain from separation from God was so intense we moved it out of our awareness and pushed it away as a projection into a world what we call our "life" in a body. This hasn't happened to us as an external cause, it's come from us internally. In honest truth here, you are not "alive" in the first place, it's a projection, life being a simulation of moving images to trick us into thinking its happening to us and since this is an internal causation, the suffering doesn't go away as a release by calling on death. The mind needs to heal within.

Embodiment of fear, the host of sin, god of the guilty and the lord of all illusions and deceptions, does the thought of death seem mighty. For it seems to hold all living things within its withered hand; all hopes and wishes in its blighting grasp; all goals perceived but in its sightless eyes. The frail, the helpless and the sick bow down before its image, thinking it alone is real, inevitable, worthy of their trust. For it alone will surely come. (W-P1.163.2:1)

Jesus is describing the Ego and what we believe death is when we affiliate with our character. We have made an idol out of Death which is a replacement for God. If we identify with the Ego then we experience death because we have chosen it. He's even mentioning in the third sentence that we bow down and worship it. We believe we have killed God and destroyed our home (our kingdom). We then project the guilt on to our life and it appears as problems in various forms. If you can't see the source of the problem and you accept the problems which appear here as really happening to you then you will count on death because they wear you down as you don't release the guilt, you sustain it. Death comes as the end of all hope, wishes and goals.

> *All things but death are seen to be unsure, too quickly lost, however, hard to gain, uncertain in their outcome, apt to fail the hopes they once engendered, and to leave the taste of dust and ashes in their wake, in place of aspirations and of dreams. But death is counted on. For it will come with certain footsteps when the time has come for its arrival. It will never fail to take all life as hostage to itself.* (W-P1.163.3:1)

He continues to expand on our belief in death. We are unsure of everything else but certain on death. Our aspirations, hopes and dreams are ambiguous, but we will undoubtedly die. The purpose of the Ego is to defeat God, and death seems to be the ultimate weapon which it uses to try to convince us that it is the only thing we can be certain about. The Ego wants us to believe death is true as it would have to mean that the body is real – that our experience in the body is what life is.

> *Would you bow down to idols such as this? Here is the strength and might of God Himself perceived within an idol made of dust. Here is the opposite of God proclaimed as lord of all creation, stronger than God's Will for life, the endlessness of love and Heaven's*

perfect, changeless constancy. Here is the Will of Father and of Son defeated finally and laid to rest beneath the headstone death has placed upon the body of the holy Son of God. (W-P1.163.4:1)

To worship Death, is to worship an idol made of dust which is here to replace the strength of God. The opposite of God is worshipped, i.e. the Ego, who we believe is stronger than God's will for life. We actually believe it is stronger than God's endless love and stronger than heaven's perfect endless state. From Jesus's point of view he sees you right now as God created you, immortal, so watching us believe we can die is completely alien to the truth, you can hear it in his words, he is completely certain we cannot die. It's like convincing my toddler that Vegetables are good for her, we know it but she wants anything else but the truth! Worshipping Death is the Ego's proof that God the father and child are separated, and that their relationship is broken.

Unholy in defeat, he has become what death would have him be. His epitaph, which death itself has written, gives no name to him, for he has passed to dust. It says but this: "Here lies a witness God is dead." And this it writes again and still again, while all the while its worshippers agree, and kneeling down with foreheads to the ground, they whisper fearfully that it is so. (W-P1.163.5:1)

According to the Ego, death is where God removes this "life" from us for wanting and making this "life" of separation from him. This makes us fear God and value this "life" so much without him. Death provides evidence for us that the Ego is right after all and thus it convinces us that we cannot be the boundless perfect creation Jesus says we are. If you believe in Death, you believe that God can die. It is the final judgment of the Ego against God. It says that our bodily reality is what is real, and if the body is what is real, God's reality cannot be true. This leads to death being held up as the proof that our reality as eternal beings cannot be true. **Jesus also wants us to know that it's a choice that we have made, it's not just happening to us, but believing you can die doesn't mean you actually can, only the character you have made of you has ended, which was never who you are in the first place!** In the final sentence he's trying to show us how little we have become if we think that death is the end of us. He says this because he only sees you as you really are, everlasting.

> *It is impossible to worship death in any form, and still select a few you would not cherish and would yet avoid, while still believing in the rest. For death is total. Either all things die, or else they live and cannot die. No compromise is possible. For here again we see an obvious position, which we must accept if we be sane; what contradicts one thought entirely can not be true, unless its opposite is proven false.* (W-P1.163.6:1)

He tells us it's impossible to worship death in any form as death is total. **Total is either all things die or else they live and cannot die.** Let's look at this much closer. If death exists at all, it must *totally* contradict life, it is life's opposite. Since it comes in many forms, and we select the ones we value and the ones we would avoid in order to make it suit our preference – it cannot possibly be true. *Anger, faithlessness, sadness or anxiety are forms of death we sometimes choose and sometimes don't, so how can we partially have "life" here? By following these forms when we feel like we make the death of our character alive, to suit our liking, that is what makes this act in a play seem like a-live performance.*

When we choose these, it isn't Total, **therefore it must be the latter; to live and cannot die which is how God created us.** From the root thought of "life ending" every form "in which the wish to be as you are not" are the thoughts of death. My concern with my body and wishing to lose weight is a veiled form of a death thought. Part of the motivation to losing weight is to "live longer", but if the body is not alive at all, what are we talking about?

The idea of the death of God is so preposterous that even the insane have difficulty in believing it. For it implies that God was once alive and somehow perished; killed, apparently, by those who did not want Him to survive. Their stronger will could triumph over His, and so eternal life gave way to death. And with the Father died the Son as well. (W-P1.163.7:1)

It's absolutely insane to believe that God can die. How can the all-encompassing, omnipresent source of creation perish? It is only our own arrogance that thinks we are more powerful than God and have overcome him. The belief in death suggests that there was once a God and now we have ended its life. It's a ridiculous belief system we have identified with.

Death's worshippers may be afraid. And yet, can thoughts like these be fearful? If they saw that it is only this which they believe, they would be instantly released. And you will show them this today. There is no death, and we renounce it now in every form, for their salvation and our own as well. God made not death. Whatever form it takes must therefore be illusion. This the stand we take today. And it is given us to look past death, and see the life beyond. (W-P1.163.8:1)

We can't have life and death, life is eternal and changeless, both are opposed and clearly you can't have both with no compromise. We have simply lost our awareness of the truth of who we really are as everlasting beings. It's not real and is just an illusionary belief we hold.

Our Father, bless our eyes today. We are Your messengers, and we would look upon the glorious reflection of Your Love which shines in everything. We live and move in You alone. We are not separate from Your eternal life. There is no death, for death is not Your Will. And we abide where You have placed us, in the life we share with You and with all living things, to be like You and part of You forever. We accept Your Thoughts as ours, and our will is one with Yours eternally. (W-P1.163.9:1)

We do not see what is there because we are blinded by the littleness that we think we are. The more we study *A Course in Miracles* the more experiences we get that death is a concept, that there is no Ego; but we made the Ego in believing in it and we can dispel it by not believing in it. The Ego itself is a death wish. Self-Realization is the mind removing all that we are not to reveal what has always been there – eternal life. We can't die because we were created by God as eternal. There's only the Ego trick to convince us we are flesh, time creatures that we are bound between birth and death.

The solution is simple, follow your higher self with forgiveness and all illusions will fade. We will grow out of our worldly desires, so we won't crave experiences, which is a form of suffering as it takes away our peace. We peel away all the Ego with the intensity of awareness to our inner Joy. Through this process of dissolving, we can all meet God as one and reach a state of Moksha which ends the cycle of birth and death.

To reach this state of liberation we need to understand the difference between form over content or the body over the mind. The body is not alive so it cannot die. It's a projection of the Ego mind. What happens when I leave the body? The course teaches you are never in the body, you are always in the decision-making part of your mind dreaming you are in a body, dreaming that it was born into a certain time interval and dreaming that the body died. All the while this dream is occurring you are in your mind, so the answer to what happens when you die is nothing, because nothing happened while you were here. Think of yourself watching a movie at the cinema in a nice comfortable seat. For three hours your brain is somewhere else, your identified with the characters, the scenes, events in the movie, then the movie finishes. In the movie some people live and some die, some are hurt and some are happy. Has anything changed in you? No, you are still sitting in your seat for those three hours, you joined the filmmaker's dream and you identified with the characters on the screen, the movie ends. You never left your seat. Then you say, "I want to watch another movie," so you change screens, you never leave your seat again and the next three hours in the movie you're in another time and place with different characters but you never left your seat. Similarly when we are dreaming a dream of living and dying we never left our decision-making seat so whichever teaching Guide (Holy Spirit or Ego) is still there in my mind when I watch the movie is still there when the body dies. You don't have sudden visions when you die. You don't necessarily see a white light when you die, you may or you may not. If you die and you are wrong minded you will have wrong-minded thoughts; if you die and are right minded you have right-minded thoughts. When I say Wrong, I mean identifying with thoughts of what you are not, right mind is associating with unification, wholeness and our eternal being. Nothing is here, nothing changes. What changes is your decision to be with the Holy Spirit or the Ego; that's what changes.

Example of Death's Forms

As I write this chapter on Death, Guruji brings a live example into my perception of many forms of death this morning on a work team call. As mentioned above from the root thought of "life ending" different forms appear – sadness, fear, anxiety, lack of trust, concern for the body. All forms in which the wish to be as you are not are alternatives on the thought of death. At this point in time I had been working from home in a Coronavirus pandemic for 18 months, the nation went into a national lockdown and it seemed that the world was now slowly opening up. I had a team call in the morning so I logged on, and out of the blue my boss tells everyone that we will be going back into the office two days a week starting in two weeks' time. As I heard this news, I felt a wave of thoughts of sadness, fear, anxiety, lack of trust, and concern for the body flood my mind. We have a great system in place to take care of the baby, how will this work out? Going in by train is more expensive and my wife is on maternity leave next year with another baby to arrive. Will this reduce our savings for their future? Travelling into work will take three hours out of my day; I won't get to see my child after work if I leave at 5:30pm. All of the ways I have made the last 18 months work for me were being reversed, but it was my choice to decide how I feel about this. After all I am the decision-making mind here. There was another call with another team shortly after and I brought the topic up. This team didn't have to come in two days a week as their leader didn't feel it was necessary but said that my functional leader wants all of the team in work. Suddenly another wave of thoughts came through, which tried to make the leader the villain and myself the victim. This was a fantastic experience for me. I was able to see right through all of this. I immediately forgave myself for this situation, the leader for what he has not done and my boss for being the messenger. They were showing me the separation from God which I believed in my mind. It was being projected onto dream characters including Akash so I can make them guilty for this situation. The Ego wants me to attack and hate them, to be sad, fearful, anxious, concerned about the survival of my body and mostly to not have trust in my Creator. I thanked Guru-Je for this blessed vision and all the sonship for giving me *A Course in Miracles* in order to see what is there. To give an analogy, the dark clouds came to cover the endless sky of what I am but I chose to stay silent and watch them rather than identify with them and become angry, sad or concerned. I watched as they slowly passed to reveal the limitless being of what I am. I chose to not identify with these lies and remain open to what experience comes to me in the present moment of now.

To conclude this chapter, I wanted to encourage you to look up Anita Moorjani who encountered a near death experience and is living proof that the mind continues after the body ceases. Her experience after the body was within the split mind of consciousness. When she was explaining her encounter outside of the body, she also explains what being in the body is like. In her everyday life the body gives experiences through a limited lens like looking at each scenario of life with a flashlight, but outside of the body it was like the floodlights come on in a giant warehouse and you become well aware of all of the mind where some things are beautiful and others that are not so nice. This is the expansive mind. We know from the course that the mind projects the body and that there is no gap between the body-mind. Her experience reaffirms this for us all.

Chapter Eight

Unified Field

*– In our world a Ne<u>two</u>rk is connecting to more than **one**; to **two**. This naturally **works** once you know you are **one** unified field networking within your own universal body. –*

A Trip to the Gym

This morning I went to the gym to work out on the cross trainer. For 10 minutes I was thinking about the next section of this book and which topic will come through next. Something that stuck with me was "Unified Field". I'm no scientist so I asked Guru-Je again as I finished my workout and got down from the machine. I looked up and saw the back of a man's T-shirt, which was a Barcelona football team shirt, and the benefactor was "UNICEF". As I stared at it, he put the word "Unified Field" back into my mind. So, I knew my next topic was this.

What is the Unified Field?

We have an unlimited field of awareness, where consciousness is aware of itself alone – science calls this the unified field. This is where it appears that everything is one and everything is many at the very same time. We are the one child of God, but also, we are appearing as many Children of God at the same time. There is only one Being and hence one Mind, and there are also seemingly many minds in the one Being.

The split mind is a mind divided against itself, in which the more aware half is fenced off from its own true nature by denial, fear and dissociation. This split, which is illusionary and not real, is then projected outward and symbolized by a split between the mind and other minds. In this divided state, the mind cannot truly create or communicate, for what it generates is uncertain and inconsistent.

The course describes the primary split mind as between the separated mind and Christ's mind. The secondary split is within the separated mind between thought systems of The Ego or The Holy Spirit; the Holy Spirit is our guide out of the split. The separated mind is holding all of the physical parts in place like when a TV plays a movie it enables the moving picture to occur on the screen through pixels. Then through the actors, script, scenes, and words the moving picture is created with different scenes depending on whether you choose the Holy Spirit or the Ego.

In Truth, there is no detachment between these minds, only the Mind of God exists. However, there is a veil that appears to show us that the Mind is fragmented into conscious parts projecting out physical bodies and objects. The body is not a container or a housing for the mind. The body is an effect of the Mind which is the cause. Underneath the veil there is no dividing line between minds. There's no place where one ends and another begins, and so our "life" is really the separated mind, projecting out all bodies and objects.

Science tells us that the unified field has its origins in a non-local space in the form of indestructible and not directly observable wave functions. These wave functions which store all aspects of consciousness in the form of information are always present in and around the body. Reflecting on this interrelated nature of creation, the universe works more like a magnificent celestial hologram. In a hologram every portion of whatever the object is contains that object in its entirety, only on a smaller scale. What we see as our world is actually the projection of something that's happening at a deeper level of creation. In this view of "above, below" and "within, without", patterns are contained within patterns complete in and of themselves and different only in scale.

Now we can see the interconnectedness of what we are to everything. When something is completely unified how can there be guilt and anger amongst itself? How can we have interpersonal problems or family conflicts, rivalry, wars with each other when there actually is only one of us? It's unreal, and since it's not real how can you blame "them" for it when "they" are you? Surely we would only love ourself and forgive ourself for what we have not done.

How it Connects all of Us

I have experienced so many ways of how we are so interconnected. I remember when we were all in a National Lockdown in the UK from the COVID-19 virus, and the first year we had a small window of time, maybe a couple of months in the summer, to go out and have a domestic holiday. My wife gave it to me to organize as she wanted to make something of her maternity leave, and it was baby's first-ever holiday. I quite rightfully gave it all to Guru-Je to arrange. First to understand was where to go. The destination came into my mind from a family member, which is the unified field linking its parts; this person spoke to my wife about having visited the Cotswolds, so it came into my awareness from another part of the field, my wife. The Cotswolds is a big place with many options available, so I opened my mind up ready for what idea he had planned. I went online and was then navigated to a picture which I thought was very beautiful; it was a river with bridges in Bourton-on-the-Water. He then guided me to stay at a particular hotel as it had a large family room available, and being vegetarian had an Italian restaurant inside which many other hotels didn't, where you needed to go to the strip outside to get food. The entire trip was fantastic, and I knew it was planned by Guruji because everything was thought of, the layout of the room was perfect where we could put baby to sleep far enough so she wouldn't see us and want to join us in bed, but not far enough that we would be worried about her. There were ideal things to do with Birdland, a mini Model Village of the area and the Dragonfly Maze, none of these I did much research on at all. There happened to be lots of parents with babies of a similar age. There was a couple who paid for my wife's drinks because she was deprived of any holidays in a national lockdown year in her maternity leave, and there were all my favorite treats, a sweet shop with local fudge, an ice cream parlor and a burger place that sells vegan burgers. The waiter at this burger place was so friendly that it was like I knew him from a previous life. It was like the unified field was connecting us to him in order to have a beautiful experience.

Another way that Guru-Je connects me to the best outcome is by sometimes preventing what I desire from happening to give me a much more loving and beneficial path from the one I wanted to bring forth. He really wants me to surrender into the Holy instant or the present moment where I don't think of the nonexistent future and don't dwell into the nonexistent past. The year after this fantastic trip we also had another opportunity for a holiday, and this time I really wanted to go to the same place again. Akash the person wanted to relive the past into the future which of course is the Ego. So I called the hotel up, and to my surprise all of the rooms for the month were fully booked. I then spoke to my wife and I was met with resistance. We were expecting another baby and she was in her first trimester so morning sickness put her off any holiday bookings. The next day we took our child to the shopping mall and she was an absolute nightmare to handle. She was like a kid in a candy store picking everything up from the shelves, trying to open unpaid products and running into people. Then the thought arose into me, which was the unified field connecting itself with its wider self, how will she be able to be in a place like Bourton-on-the Water with rivers and bridges everywhere. She's not the little baby in a sling a year on and we might not enjoy a trip like this. With all of these blockages plus the cost of the same stay more than doubling a year on, I surrendered to the moment and gave gratitude to the Holy Spirit who prevented me from taking an Arduous path or a wasted time. Always watch for problematic behavior in your surroundings. It's telling you that there is a version of you who has had that experience in the future, and you didn't like it so don't try to force the situation, surrender to the Holy instant.

Another way the unified field connects its components together is making life seem difficult to make you feel like it's falling apart when really it's coming together. Before the job that I am in now, which was guided to me by Guruji, he had to give me some motivation to want to move to the next classroom to teach me in. So, the unified mind creates this motivation through experiences with people and changes in situation. Firstly, I was made to feel underpaid. I knew I was doing a job which two people were doing on a higher salary banding. This was frustrating, and although I was tolerating it well with my modesty the unified mind was constantly connecting me to people who were going up the work ladder and getting promotions or being part of the leader's succession planning. Secondly the workload was tremendous; I even came into work on a bank holiday to finish off the reporting. Finally a couple of internal moves never worked out for me, even one that with was my friend who could have become my manager. I managed to fail the interview as I was not myself but behaved like I thought he wanted me to be. It felt like my work life was falling apart, when really it was coming together. There was literally only one path in front of me, moving externally in Guruji's job. None of that worked for me because the unified field had me connected to all the amazing people to meet and great work I was to do in this new place. The package was great, and I was at the level I felt I should be. Looking back he was just making me feel comfortable with the package and level in order to sit in his classroom with lots of lessons coming my way. Although this level at work is an illusion the Holy Spirit was using what the Ego made to purify the mind. The money was his to manage, the workload was his to distribute, the work relationships were his to handle. I was only there for the lessons to be learnt through forgiveness.

Everything we do is related to everything else. The unified field is fully connected to all of its parts. To increase our awareness of this network we can connect directly to the one who is fully part of the network. Guruji or Jesus will navigate us through it by paving the path to our next adventure. If you have a question, just ask; you don't need to dig for answers, the answers will emerge. They arise through sudden insight or an unplanned creative experience. Perhaps you will meet a person who is somehow related to the coincidence; a discussion, an encounter, a relationship, or a circumstance will give us a eureka moment for us to know how it is all linked. Even the passerby in the park is part of the unified field, listen closely to their words spoken, look at the words on their clothes or accessories, are they jogging to instigate your exercise after a heavy Christmas food intake? Do they remind you of someone you need to forgive? Just "be" in the now and say to yourself, "There I go on a different adventure" – enjoy being with yourself.

Coincidences

Coincidences are a huge part of the unified field. Coincidences are here all the time but many of us do not connect the dots and just think it's chance. At my new workplace we were never in a fixed seat for our roles, we had to book a weekly slot in any seat in the building a week prior to arriving. It was amazing how the Holy Spirit communicated to me. One time I sat near a group of Human Resource colleagues and the words coming out of their mouths had a different meaning to me than it did in their conversation. I once had a problem faced my way from a colleague and it was very challenging to solve. The man opposite was on a phone call and he said, "Actually reporting is part of this role specification." I understood the words "Reporting Actuals" which is the finalized financial figures, and I knew my answer was in that file. I found the sheet in the Excel file and managed to solve my colleague's issue. Another time I was sitting next to someone who was awfully silent. We sat together for two weeks in a row, and I turned to him to try to have a chat. He saw the book I was reading from my laptop bag, which was *The Disappearance of the Universe* by Gary Renard, and he said, "That sounds interesting. Is it spiritual?" To my amazement we actually had so much in common. He had actually heard of *A Course in Miracles*, and said he wasn't ready for it yet, but we held so many conversations on the observer effect, the holographic universe and our perceptions leading to the unreality of the world. We were sat next to a meeting room and we discussed the observer effect, said that behind that door there's endless possibilities, we all see a different room. We may use the same human made-up words to describe it but that limits what is there. He asked me why the room is so similar for each of us and I mentioned it's because we are all part of the same consciousness, and it's the collective mind that creates the scene. Wave functions which store all aspects of consciousness in the form of information are always present, and the act of observing will influence the phenomenon being observed, for example for us to see an electron, a photon must first interact with it and this interaction will change the path of that electron. Meeting a likeminded person in such a random way and having a conversation with them, which was unlike any other conversation I have had, was the unified field attracting itself to itself.

Although the cosmos is an illusion it's unwise to dismiss it as trivial. The phenomenal universe operates according to inbuilt intelligence. When any form is created, it functions according to the pre-encoded template provided by this deeper level of creation. It's a storehouse of knowledge. Whether it is plant knowledge, people knowledge, mind or matter knowledge, it creates out of itself and provides the intelligence for all life to thrive according to set patterns. The universe governs and manages everything, setting and upholding the laws of creation. These laws are universal and can't be violated. They aren't open to negotiation. It's an impersonal creative force. Just as the water falls on all beings in the same way, the laws of creation apply equally to all beings. If two people fall out of a plane, one a criminal and one a saint, neither will be exempted from gravity, there's no discrimination. The system is an orderly and intelligently-designed matrix.

Since we have limited ourselves within this grand design, we need assistance. Jesus says in the course:

A split mind cannot perceive its fullness, and needs the miracle of its wholeness to dawn upon it and heal it. This reawakens the wholeness in it, and restores it to the Kingdom because of its acceptance of wholeness. The full appreciation of the mind's Self-fullness makes selfishness impossible and extension inevitable. That is why there is perfect peace in the Kingdom. (T-7.9.4:3)

The principle of superposition is an example of this intelligence. It's the ability of objects to appear in multiple positions at the same time. We see from our next chapter on perception how little we have made ourselves, and then we look at the space-time continuum which builds us back up to the vastness of what we are.

Chapter Nine

Perception & the Space-Time Continuum

*– A Cal**end**ar is here to show us time exists. If we remove the effects that illusionary time has on us, we can remove the other letters to reveal the **End** of time. In fact, Consciousness is the **Lend-Ar** of time to that which is all. –*

Distorted Perception

Let's begin with what Jesus says about the problems that we perceive:

Let me recognize the problem so it can be solved. A problem cannot be solved if you do not know what it is. Even if it is really solved already you will still have the problem, because you will not recognize that it has been solved. This is the situation of the world. The problem of separation, which is really the only problem, has already been solved. Yet the solution is not recognized because the problem is not recognized. (W-P1.79.1:1)

Let me recognize my problems have been solved. (W-P1.80.1:1)

In the course, Jesus shows us that we have a cracked perception, that what we perceive is a distorted interpretation from our inner mind. He describes to us very clearly that we do not even know what the problem is. We think problems are outside in the world, the tree falling on the roof, the car accident, the abuser, a global virus, wars between nations – there are millions of problems here. He tells us in plain English that these forms are not the actual problem. There's only one problem, the belief in the separation from God. We keep ourselves so mindlessly focusing on the roof, the car accident, the abuser, the virus, the wars, that we can't perceive the root issue here. This is what is meant by our perception is distorted or cracked. The problem is the separation from God, but we are so lost in the game of life that we can't see through the lie in order to hand it over to the Holy Spirit for release. When we say it has already been corrected, we mean the Holy Spirit has guaranteed the release of guilt from every single possible variation of problems in time. It sees all of time as a simultaneous moment of now and ensures our way back home. From this moment in time, if we can correct our perception through continued forgiveness of all our problems and hand it over to Guru-Je, he reduces time to the point where there is no more need for time.

So now we know the solution is here, it's not going to help you at all if you miss to define the problem. Similarly, if we have a nail to put into the wall and the solution given is a screwdriver it's not going to be of great help. If you think you have financial problems, environmental problems, health problems, interpersonal problems etc. the temptation to keep the problem of separation remains unsolved. By perceiving only one problem in many, you would understand that you have the means to solve them all. And you would use the means because you recognize the problem.

Vision – Sight

What I see reflects a process in my mind, which starts with my idea of what I want. From there, the mind makes up an image of the thing the mind desires, judges valuable, and therefore seeks to find. These images are then projected outward, looked upon, esteemed as real and guarded as one's own.
(W-PII.325.1:1)

I remember when my wife and I went on our final holiday abroad together before our first baby was born. It's called a

Babymoon and we chose Dubai. We were in a luxurious pool and the setting was lavish, except for one side where a large building was being built. My wife stared at it and said,

"That's completely ruining our surroundings, it's such a shame."

I stared at it and thought I'd start an interesting topic now I had her alone away from our busy London life. I said to her:

"Did you know that every person sees a different perception of an object?"

I knew she was very intellectual on material life subjects, but wanted to keep the topic away from the obvious ugliness of the apparent building and continue to see if her mind opened up to my thinking, I continued:

"If 7 billion people queued up to enter this pool and explained to us what they saw of that so-called 'building' every single viewpoint would be different. One would think it's going to be a marvelous expensive resort, one would think it's an ugly construction site, another person who is in the construction business would think a good job was being done and another wouldn't, another may be amazed at how such glamourous buildings are actually made, another may cast their eyes on the workers and be astonished how hard they work in 40 degree heat, one person may look at it and think it's a lovely home if they lived in meagre accommodation in a poor country maybe – literally 7 billion people would be looking at the 'building' and experiencing something different."

We may think these are just opinions from different people, maybe they use different words to describe it and that the actual object is the same for everyone. Let's go into this deeper as that's not true. The object only exists in our own personal experience of it. We would firstly all try to use our human fabricated words to describe it – "an ugly, dusty grey building" – this would come from the Ego which veils the truth and obscures your vision with your past. It's ugly because it must resemble something unattractive that you have experienced in the past, or it doesn't meet your idea of beauty which your mind has constructed and concluded arbitrarily. It has selected out what it regards as attractive and misses the beauty in what it doesn't see. As they say, beauty is in the eyes of the beholder. We only see the past in any object. If you remove all ideas of your past in shapes, colors, numbers, letters, memories, experience, words and beliefs, you will be able to look at something and see what is – a part of you within consciousness. This is the now. Emptying out your mind of concepts and ideas. I thought I'd now extend the conversation further to see her reaction,

"If 7 billion people are having a different experience with the object and seeing what they want, what is the object?"

She looked at me and smiled. She had no answer. I continued,

"Your beliefs give you your perspective, this gives you your perception which is basically your interpretation of what you see, and this then finally provides you with what you experience. If you change your belief, you change your experience and as you change your experience with the object, you see in the object what you want to see, not what is apparently there as there is nothing there except what you perceive. So, we all actually see a different Truth."

For most of my life before I was 30 I believed eating mainly meat in my diet would give me bigger muscles through protein, and vegetables were for the less physically stronger people. I then changed my belief and moved to eating only vegetables. In changing my belief I completely changed my experience, and the object of meat supplying me protein left my awareness and was replaced by a collection of objects in vegetables. Did the meat and protein exist? Only in my experience of it, which was temporary and in the past, which is now nonexistent, so no. This is why when you eat the same food over again you have different experiences. For e.g. the same type of apple might not be as juicy, or as flavorsome to you. It's not because this new apple is unique and separate to everything else, it's because so many intricate variables are changing my state of mind now. All of the millions of intelligent cells in my body are working together differently compared to when I last ate the same apparent apple, not to mention the enormous field of particles interacting in so many ways everywhere and all of the time. This allows the experience I am having with this apple now to happen once only ever. It's the Ego's veil that covers us with ignorance that we miss life's most beautiful encounters which is sourced from the mind. The apple is consciousness as is our body, and this encounter is creative energy interacting with itself. I went on:

"If you have a conditioned mind which is knowledgeable on the construction industry you will have a firm belief rooted into your mind and will interpret what you see with more in-depth thoughts on the subject matter; e.g., if you're a safety manager on the construction site you will have a wider opinion on what you see because that is what you are looking for and so that will be your interpretation and so what you experience. So the object becomes what you want it to be. It's not there as a fixed object separate to consciousness. If the same person changes careers and becomes a hotel manager and could look upon the same construction site, he will be looking at the site as a potential job opening one day which he can manage and so will have a completely different experience."

So, what is the object and what is our world? It's not 7 billion different people seeing one fixed world which is apart from them. It's one consciousness reflecting 7 billion worlds from it. But if each world is different, why is there consistency of the same earth? Because we all come from the same consciousness, your world is private, *objects don't have existence, existence has objects.* Every object appears in awareness within the ocean of consciousness, and through our perceptions and thought, we think it into existence. We have forgotten or ignored the median

111

in which it arises and think it is already there. The actual image belongs to consciousness.

> *You live by symbols. You have made up names for everything you see. Each one becomes a separate entity, identified by its own name. By this you carve it out of unity. By this you designate its special attributes, and set it off from other things by emphasizing space surrounding it. This space you lay between all things to which you give a different name; all happenings in terms of place and time; all bodies which are greeted by a name. This space you see as setting off all things from one another is the means by which the world's perception is achieved. You see something where nothing is, and see as well nothing where there is unity; a space between all things, between all things and you. Thus do you think that you have given life in separation. By this split you think you are established as a unity which functions with an independent will. What are these names by which the world becomes a series of discrete events, of things ununified, of bodies kept apart and holding bits of mind as separate awarenesses? You gave these names to them, establishing perception as you wished to have perception be. The nameless things were given names, and thus reality was given them as well. For what is named is given meaning and will then be seen as meaningful; a cause of true effect, with consequence inherent in itself.* (W-P1.184.1:1)

The mind projects everything, sees its own projection from a distinct and seemingly separate viewpoint and then interprets that perception as an external fact. The body being the object as an experience of separation. We see the universe through our own perception. The one mind of God has an appearance of being split into the Ego and the Holy Spirit; this is consciousness. The fragmented mind then superimposes limitation through a median of perception and thought, thus we have an experience of being small and part of something grander, when actually we are the grandness. It's an illusion, a veil covering the enormity of what we are. Through the Holy Spirit's awakening our perception is corrected and our awareness is heightened. We are freer and less tied down to the heavy burdens of this world. *One thing that is vital and you can't take off if you don't realize this – you must realize that you have a perceptual problem because you have chosen the Ego's thought system.* The Ego is likely to strongly deny this and remind you of your apparent abilities and skills. It does this to weaken you, to limit you so you keep following its delusional thinking. It can also use it the other way to directly deflate you and belittle you so you think there is something wrong with you, and to make you suffer. Remember you only have a perceptual problem because you affiliate with the Ego which clouds your unlimited sky. The thing to do is admit you have a perceptual problem because you chose the wrong teacher, and to give your perception to the Holy Spirit which unifies perceptions. Jesus will never give up on us and gives it to us straight up in the opening 10 workbook lessons of *A Course in Miracles*. He directly identifies our perceptual problem:

Nothing I see means anything
I have given what I see all the meaning it has for me
I do not understand anything I see
These thoughts do not mean anything
I am never upset for the reason I think.
I am upset because I see something that is not there.
I see only the past
My mind is preoccupied with past thoughts.
I see nothing as it is now.
My thoughts do not mean anything.
(W-P1.1-10.1:1)

The truth is only an infinite being can perceive reality exactly how it's happening; also he cannot explain it in words because words cannot describe space and time. He can only tell you to wait for it to become your own experience.

The Act of Observation collapses possibility into reality

An electron is a particle, but where is the location of the electron? Since it is a wave, what is the speed of the wave? The wave particle can be either a wave or a particle or even both at the same time. But you cannot determine both the location and the speed of the electron at the same time because the very act of observing the location of the electron will change its speed, and the very act of determining the speed of the electron will change its location. This is known in science as the Heisenberg Uncertainty Principle. When we see, we see through our personal conditioned mind, i.e. our biased and deep-rooted memories. All of a person's act of observation is covered by his own conditioning; based on that he makes the happening suit his own experience of reality. In the case of the particle wave, the very act of observing "collapses" the wave particle to a particle or wave. Wave functions which store all aspects of consciousness in the form of information are always present, and the act of observing will affect the phenomenon that is observed, for us to see an electron, a photon must first interact with it and this interaction will change the path of that electron. Please look up the double-slit experiment which proves that the very act of observation changes the possibility into a particular reality. I can confirm that if you choose the Holy Spirit in any problematic situation it will give you the unified possibility and that will be the reality you experience. By choosing forgiveness you are choosing to see this situation with God's love and it will be beautiful. Living a life of this leads to a happy dream which leads to waking up in our true state inside the kingdom of God. If you choose the Ego, you will experience loneliness, isolation, anger, frustration, and guilt. It's your choice at every moment.

Space-Time Continuum

In our world we live in a three-dimensional plane, fundamentally made up of the five basic elements – earth, fire, water, space, and air. Within our section of time the objects that we perceive appear to be created, maintained, and dissolved back into the ecosystem around us. We think we are the bodies within this world and use our five senses to experience it – sight, hearing, taste, smell and touch. This gives us a very limited experience as we do not understand the extent of what we are. Once we logically understand our grandeur, we can realize the options available to us and life will not be problematic. As an example, if we knew the enormity of our richness would we fight and argue with another over money, would we unnecessarily seek popularity, or mindlessly focus the majority of life on career progression? You wouldn't burgle a home for money, you wouldn't judge another based on their social circles and you wouldn't work all day and night for false power in your career if you knew your greatness. We wouldn't approach it in that way at all if we knew the options available to us and the possibilities accessible at our fingertips. Life here is about understanding the magnitude of our being. In our linear world when you are seven years old you play with a toy car, when 17 you want a real car, when 27 a different type of car etc. Our civilization calls this growth. By Intellectually understanding the grandness of our being we can make our lives much more enriched than from these superficial methods. Our small self (what we think we are) is nothing but a mental construct. Some of us think they are big business advisors or managers, others think they are successful leaders in a field, others believe they are highly trained professionals or very successful athletes. We say, "I am this or I am that," but actually if we stopped at "I" the rest of the words after add no triumph to you, in fact they reduce your magnificence. When we know the enormity of our richness, then when a thought comes into our mind the entire unified field works together to make it happen as everything vibrates with you. This is about integrating this discrete, individual you with the rest of you and then radiating this breakthrough. Understanding this magnificence breaks down the barriers you have set up around you and expands your awareness.

Let's discuss the vastness of what we are by firstly looking at the dimensions of our universe.

Dimensions

1 Dimension

Point   Point Marks a Line   Line

Take a point, a one-dimensional object; when a point marks across a path, it creates a line. A one-dimensional being perceives a world as an infinite number of points in the same direction.

2 Dimensions

Now let's look at marking the movement of a line, a two-dimensional object. If it just moves in the same direction then obviously it will just continue to be a line, however, if it moves in a direction which is not within in it, it creates a surface or a plane. A two-dimensional being perceives a world as an infinite number of lines.

3 Dimensions

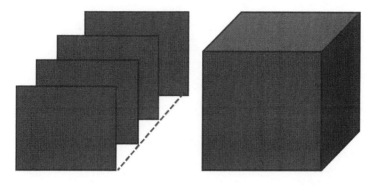

In the same way, if a surface of a plane moves in a direction which is not within it, it will mark a solid, three-dimensional object. A three-dimensional being perceives a world as an infinite number of surfaces. As a three-dimensional being, we have more line of sight of what we are perceiving. There's Height, Width and Depth to our objects.

As we move to these higher dimensions from lower dimensions, we see the lower dimensions as slices of a higher dimensional area. In our three-dimensional world, fingers perceived by us are fully connected to the hand. Suppose a horizontal plane intersects the beginning of the fingers. Now on this plane, all the sections of the fingers seem to be all separate and not connected to each other. But from the three-dimensional space we can see these are all sections of the fingers of the single hand. In a 2D view, if we were to hurt one finger we would think it doesn't impact the other fingers. When in fact the entire hand is adversely affected and suffers. Similarly if we massage one finger with love and care, it brings pleasure to the whole hand.

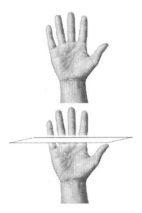

4 Dimensions

Equally, we can imagine a four-dimensional area as an infinite number of three-dimensional areas. In the four-dimensional world, we call the fourth dimension "time" – the space-time continuum. We recognize time in three ways, past, present and future. From our viewpoint the past has already happened and doesn't exist any longer, the future is still to experience so does not exist, and the present is an emergence after a nonexistent past and from a nonexistent future. In the three-dimensional world we see the fingers connected as a hand; similarly, we can assume a collective consciousness that exists beyond our plane of life. Those with four-dimensional vision see the continuity in the fourth dimension of time with the past, present and future all existing all together. This collective consciousness sees all experiences which the individual consciousness sees as separate experiences split up by periods of time. A three-dimensional person who is moving through time marks a four-dimensional being. Along time, we can see the movement into a path as we grow from baby to teenager to adult to an older body. But we cannot see, feel or fully experience this fourth dimensional being because of our restricted perception. In our three-dimensional world we only see a slice of the fourth dimensional being, which is the normal three-dimensional person. It's like when I snip a single image from a video on my phone, you don't see the entire video in moving continuation, just a particular part of it.

From a two-dimensional person's perspective, it's impossible to believe that there can exist events or experiences beyond his plane of perception. So, to recognize the three-dimensional world he must rise to the three-dimensional consciousness. In the same way, to realize the fourth dimensional world we need to be in the fourth dimensional consciousness. Which is very much possible by constantly being in the present moment with the higher self – which Holy forgiveness brings you into through the miracle. Our life here – what we believe as reality through everyday living – is a fragmented existence. It is only a perception of events being distinct in space-time. Our very perception of the world itself is uncertain the deeper we look at it. We don't see what is there, we see what appears as our experience which is dependent on the lens of consciousness we see with. If it's a high-grade lens then we see with the Divine's vision. Following Guru-Je will lead us to the sight of our true self; The Child of God.

So, from our small point of view, the Cosmos is vast and gigantic, and everything was projected outward in an instant. It covers every single possibility of consciousness, all our past, present and future lives in different forms, and then also the unlimited possibilities of branching futures as our different selves making different decisions. All of this is happening at once from the position of the absolute reality, and it was all over in an instant from the perspective of the absolute reality. In *A Course in Miracles* Jesus states that God did not create this, because the cosmos is duality, the belief that there is light and darkness, that there is high and low, up and down, that there is God and us separate. The one Child of God wanted to experience what it was like to be an "I", a "self", and so aligned with the Ego thought system and is dreaming an entire cosmos of possibilities in order to experience a "self-concept" over and over again in different forms. You are this child of God, the dreamer of the dream not the dream figure with self-concepts in space-time. You have been created perfectly in the mind of God, but now have a split mind of the Holy Spirit (the remembrance of what we are) and the Ego (false self). The Ego mind created a veil that masks the fact that you are a decision-making mind. You are so grand that you can change your perceptions, outlook and future states to be peaceful, joyful and united with all of the other parts of yourself. At every moment if you completely follow the Holy Spirit all the time, the Ego will fade and eventually disappear. This ultimately leads to the cosmos disappearing as we wake up to be inside the mind of God.

Your Guru is an inner symbol that you will use to build a trustworthy relationship with to attain your higher self which you chose to give away as you entered a dream state. This is a simple process to follow as you keep choosing Guru-Je, but is not an easy path to follow at first as the Ego does not want to let you go. You have chosen to believe the Ego's thought system for so long, for so many lives and your mind is conditioned. We can now choose to not believe in it, to overlook it and follow the path to freedom, liberation, Moksha and Nirvana. *There will be moments when the Ego will put a gun to your chest, but remember you don't have a chest, instead you are an immortal chest of treasure created by the supreme.* It may appear we are at war with ourselves, but our opponent isn't there; we just believe it is and can unbelieve it also. You have chosen a special time in the continuum to serve your brother and forgive him for what he hasn't done. When you choose the Universal mind, the Guru adjusts space-time and gives you a happy dream, one with Peace, Love and Joy. God doesn't wake up its child who is having a nightmare, it awakens through a happy dream. As we listen to the voice of God (the Holy Spirit) this happy dream then blends back into the absolute reality in God's mind as if the nightmare never happened; in fact it was all over in an instant. We then return to our perfect, eternal, sinless, joyful changeless state outside of space-time. To conclude the Space-Time Continuum, let's read what *A Course in Miracles* says about it:

Jesus on Time

The ego has a strange notion of time, and it is with this notion that your questioning might well begin. The ego invests heavily in the past, and in the end believes that the past is the only aspect of time that is meaningful. Remember that its emphasis on guilt enables it to ensure its continuity by making the future like the past, and thus avoiding the present. By the notion of paying for the past in the future, the past becomes the determiner of the future, making them continuous without an intervening present. For the ego regards the present only as a brief transition to the future, in which it brings the past to the future by interpreting the present in past terms. "Now" has no meaning to the ego. The present merely reminds it of past hurts, and it reacts to the present as if it were the past. The ego cannot tolerate release from the past, and although the past is over, the ego tries to preserve its image by responding as if it were present. It dictates your reactions to those you meet in the present from a past reference point, obscuring their present reality. In effect, if you follow the ego's dictates you will react to your brother as though he were someone else, and this will surely prevent you from recognizing him as he is. And you will receive messages from him out of your own past because, by making it real in the present, you are forbidding yourself to let it go. You thus deny yourself the message of release that every brother offers you now. The shadowy figures from the past are precisely what you must escape. They are not real and have no hold over you unless you bring them with you. They carry the spots of pain in your mind, directing you to attack in the present in retaliation for a past that is no more. And this decision is one of future pain. Unless you learn that past pain is an illusion, you are choosing a future of illusions and losing the many opportunities you could find for release in the present. The ego would preserve your nightmares and prevent you from awakening and understanding they are past. Would you recognize a holy encounter if you are merely perceiving it as a meeting with your own past? For you would be meeting no one, and the sharing of salvation, which makes the encounter holy, would be excluded from your sight. The Holy Spirit teaches that you always meet yourself, and the encounter is holy because you are. The ego teaches that you always encounter your past, and because your dreams were not holy, the future cannot be, and the present is without meaning. It is evident that the Holy Spirit's perception of time is the exact opposite of the ego's. The reason is equally clear, for they perceive the goal of time as diametrically opposed. The Holy Spirit interprets time's purpose as rendering the need for time unnecessary. He regards the function of time as temporary, serving only His teaching function, which is temporary by definition. His emphasis is therefore on the only aspect of time that can extend to the infinite, for now is the closest approximation of eternity that this world offers. It is in the reality of "now," without past or future, that the beginning of the appreciation of eternity lies. For only "now" is here, and only "now" presents the opportunities for the holy encounters in which salvation can be found. The ego, on the other hand, regards the function of time as one of extending itself in place of eternity, for like the Holy Spirit, the ego interprets the goal of time as its own. The continuity of past and future, under its direction, is the only purpose the ego perceives in time, and it closes over the present so that no gap in its own continuity can occur. Its continuity, then, would keep you in time, while the Holy Spirit would release you from it. It is his interpretation of the means of salvation that you must learn to accept, if you would share his goal of salvation for you. You, too, will interpret the function of time as you interpret yours. If you accept your function in the world of time as one of healing, you will emphasize only the aspect of time in which healing can occur. Healing cannot be accomplished in the past. It must be accomplished in the present to release the future. This interpretation ties the future to the present and extends the present rather than the past. But if you interpret your function as destruction, you will lose sight of the present and hold on to the past to ensure a destructive future. And time will be as you interpret it, for of itself it is nothing. (T-13.5.4:1)

So, the past is nonexistent, the future is nonexistent, and the present moment is all there is. The only use which the past has is that the Holy Spirit can utilize it for forgiveness. At the start for me this came in huge waves, where I spent lots of time being reminded of so many memories where I could have forgiven but at the time I chose to align with the Ego. It was a time of deep contemplation, surrender and gratitude to Guru-Je for seeing me as I really am despite behaving in an unloving way. To have never looked at me with fault and to have only seen me as God created me can only be greeted with great respect. As I searched my mind for every image I could bring up, I forgave each one. Some memories were tough to forgive but I did my best and gave it to Jesus. All sorts of memories arose, which I did not even think I remembered. Moments when I shouted back at my parents, when I answered back my teachers in junior school, even playing foolish pranks on my siblings as a child and upset them. Lots of people I forgave were not here in the world anymore, but if I had the memory stuck in my unconscious mind then it still existed because the body is just a projection of the mind, and if these situations were not released, they would be recycled back into the separated mind which lives on after the body dies. This process lasted a few days for a couple of hour sessions in the day and mostly at night before I fell asleep. Even now sometimes I am reminded of a time of pain, and instead of moving straight into the present moment I forgive it first. So, this is the only exception to not being in the present.

If we are to perceive in a real way, we will be aware of all reality through the awareness of our own. For this to happen, reality leaves no room for error and no illusions can enter into our sight. This means that we see everyone only as you see them **now**. Removing their past is the only way to see reality. Our past reactions to them are also not there, and if it is to them that we react then we see an image of them that we made and cherish instead of them. This is completely insane. We consider it natural to use our past experience as the reference point from which to judge the now. But this is totally unnatural as it's a fantasy. This past casts a shadow to darken the present, we keep it in our mind, and this conceals their reality from our vision. Being in the Present moment feels like being born again. The Present is a Gift.

Time can release as well as imprison, depending on whose interpretation of it you use. Past, present and future are not continuous unless you force continuity on them. If you do you can make them so for you, but don't be deceived and then believe that this is how it is, as then you are believing that reality is what you want it to be and that is just delusional. If we try to anticipate the future on the basis of our past experience and try to plan for this accordingly, we are not allowing the miracle to intervene between them to free us and to be born again. A miracle allows us to see the other person without a past and so see them as born again. This releases them, and since their past is yours, we share the release.

The present is before time was. In it are all things eternal and they are one. Why would we hold the past against them when the present offers the light of unity with them and frees you of the past. The present is a still dimension of time that does not change. If we reach out to all the other parts of us (the people out there) and touch them with the touch of Christ, we are shining each other as a remembrance of our creator as we will remember him as we call forth the witnesses to his creation. As we lay aside this world, we find another. This world is bright with love which you have given it and we will be reminded of our father and his one holy child.

Time is a Mental Idea

I wanted to share a great way of softening the heavy grip time has on us. On a much grander scale we created the illusion of time with the Ego. On a more worldly viewpoint it was us who created scheduled arrangements of things to do, whether it's watching the TV within program slots, sleeping at certain times of the day, eating on the hours we choose and many more diarized events, gatherings, meetings and affairs to keep us busy so we can have some small comfort in thinking we know what is just over the horizon. We use this to track the past and to make it real to us; also to intricately plan for the future so we lose the present and stay in a dreamlike state. We call this our "life", and we are servants to time. Have you ever thought what time is that we hold so dear and swear to live by it so seriously?

We have fabricated, quite subjectively, that a *"day"* is the time it takes for our planet to make one revolution on its axis. It's subjective because we have used the Sun as a guideline to mark a turn from where we are on Earth. As Earth revolves, our experience is the Sun rises and falls from our view and then since it is always revolving, again it rises and falls. One day we realized that Earth was more than rotating, but also following an orbit around the Sun as we move through space. We thought up that it takes approximately 365.25 Earth rotations called "days" to revolve around the Sun once, we called this a "year",

however, to make up for the missing partial day we decided to change (approximately) the fourth year so it takes 366 days for Earth to orbit the Sun and we called it a *"leap year"* – but we also set the rule that if the year is divisible by 100 and not divisible by 400 then the leap year is skipped, such as 1900! Additionally, Earth is in continuous movement and the universe is expanding at a rate we do not know so we have arbitrarily taken a base point as our exact location as a reference in order to conclude one orbit of our Sun i.e. when trying to measure an object moving in an expanding circle, when is the cycle complete and what is the cycle? Since the universe is expanding it takes less time for the Earth to revolve around the Sun now than it will in the future. Moving on, we have decided to divide a day into 24 pieces and we called them *"hours"*; this name and number could have been anything we wanted. We then divided each hour into "minutes" which we decided should have 60 parts and each of those contained 60 tinier units called *"seconds"*. We then chose to break down the *"year"* into smaller parts but more than a *"day"*; we called seven days a *"week"* and then came the challenge of a *"month"*. We chose 12 months in a year and 52.14 weeks in a *"year"*; but weeks couldn't be evenly reconciled into months within a year and so we decided to allow some months to have more *"days"* than others. To further try to measure time, we created *"millennium"*, *"centuries"* and *"decades"* to allow us to track apparent movements in past time and focus attention on planning future time. This is an Ego maneuver to try to reinforce reality in our life. We now have a way to look back and bring reality in *"history"*, i.e. make the past real and relive it into the future; to miss the now. We have also invented – quite complexly – the Greenwich Meridian (GMT) as the prime meridian of the world and is the basis for the global system of time zones. Since time is here to keep our attention firmly rooted into the world, believing and living by it as the only means of existence gets us lost in the *"**Minute**-s"* – tiny details in life and we miss the whole picture. We can say a – *"**Me-rid-i-an**"* – is *"**an**"* effort to get *"**rid**"* of the real *"**i**"* and make a false *"**Me**"* in time. All of this is a manufactured mental idea of creating some sort of method for trying to measure movements through space – we have given this the name "Time". Space being a stationary field which objects pass through. Space is the creative energy which the course describes as the Mind, which is supplied to

Spirit and the Mind has thoughts which are vibrational energy.

An example that time is a mental idea came into my life when I was off for Paternity leave when my baby was born. Literally, I was not living in a scheduled time world as I was in a continuous loop with baby of nappy changing – feeding – burping – holding and comforting – patting to sleep, for a month. Time literally stopped for me during paternity leave. My eating was not arranged into breakfast, lunch and dinner; it was whenever I could possibly put something into my mouth. Sleeping was not planned for a certain time, but whenever I could drop off for a power nap. Morning showering, shaving and bathroom routines were thrown out of the window and were done when opportunity arose. Changing clothes and dressing up to go out was next to nothing as we stayed home to fulfill the process. Exercise, gym and household chores were all given a back seat to accommodate the integration of the little one into the home. I remember there were many times my phone battery died so I lost contact with clocks and people as we used the phone to play baby sleep-soothing music on loop. All of time became lost as I forgot the days of the week, and with baby being born in December Christmas came and went in this wonderful moment of now. The Sun rising and falling became our way of moving through time; it was a dancing eternal relationship with "I" and the rest of "Myself" – in the present moment. Giving life over to the Holy-Self at what can be an extremely exhausting period of life was such a wonderful way to restore freshness to tired and weary eyes. When we see with our inner being, our vision is *"Restored"*, from our fragmented position you look back on God and the *"Rest"* of you in *"Awe"*. It's *"Rest-awed"*. *I asked for rest but was given the rest!*

So, time only really exists as a construction of our mentality. Everything that's happened and will happen – is happening all at once, right now. The way to see it simply depends on your place in space. Looking at this from our home, the Kingdom of God, you could see it all, right now. We are the ones who are moving through the one moment of now, time has no movement. The truth is there is no Time and all things exist simultaneously, at once. This is what is meant in Isaiah 65:24, *"before they call, I will answer and while they are yet speaking, I will hear."* Everything is set out, all scenarios, outcomes and possibilities in one grand present moment.

Chapter Ten

The Ego

– Know you are God, don't think you arE GOd –

What is The Ego

We can clearly see that we are far, far greater than what we appear to be. In truth we are a multidimensional being who is dreaming the entire cosmos. This is how the masters like Jesus and Guruji perform the magnificent miracles which are both visible here and also invisible which correct our past and future lives because they see all of time happening at once. They see what we have done previously, why we go through what we do now, and the cause of all of it. By putting them in the driving seat they smooth our future path both in this life and after. As we allow them to unwind our Ego and release our unconscious guilt, the obstacles to peace are removed one by one to reveal what was already there, our eternal presence. So, in order to live a peaceful fuller life, we need to understand the blockages to our Joy. If we follow and identify with the Ego the result will be **Useless**, instead if we were to **Use-less** of the Ego then peace and joy will fill our lives. This chapter looks at all of the Ego's attempts to prevent us from looking inward.

The Ego is a thought system which we have chosen to identify with. There is one Ego part of our mind, which each fragmented part selects out from and creates a unique "personality" to identify with. The Ego is either individualized or collective. Individualized Ego is the image or personality which we think we are. Before we arrived in this world, we had already selected out from a vast variety of options that it provides: our body features, skills, limitations, and character the "person" will have. On top of that, the many choices of different experiences the "person" will go through are set out in the wave functions that collapse into your experience depending on your core's inner desires and beliefs. As my belief shifts from fear to love, from lost to realization, from finite to infinite my outer perceptions also shift to a loving experience.

To be very clear, let's describe our individualized Egos. We have a personalized name and a nickname to make us more special. We are a man, a woman, transgender, something else. We are Indian, English, Chinese, American, African, a mixture of a couple or of a few. We are an artist, a doctor, an accountant, a chef, a mechanic and many more by profession. We have certain skill sets which we are good at and there are those which we are not good at (implying an apparent lack in ourselves). For example, Akash is suited to office jobs, but would not suit construction work with physical types of heavy lifting every day. We have a favorite color, a special type of food/cuisine we adore most, we have hobbies which make us who we are, and sometimes these hobbies become our livelihood such as athletics and sports. We think we have a unique body just for us that encases us as a person, and we choose our tastes of this world accordingly. We may live in a small town or a large city and so affiliate with a wider collective Ego, maybe the city of Madrid, which has a wider collective Ego of the country Spain to Europe, and we all live together in the Egoic World. Notice that whatever we have selected as our personality has a seemingly opposing or rival option. E.g. I may live in Madrid because it's much better than Barcelona because of etc. I may be an Indian and being Indian is much better than being English, or vice versa. This thought system allows conflict, in fact it feeds from it to exist. Most of us think the Ego is being egotistical i.e. showing off a new big home, a fancy new car, a newly sculpted body from dieting and exercise or maybe a lifestyle which is perceived to be higher than the others. This is not the Ego, but the part of the Ego which the thought system wants you to see, and does not want you to see the rest, for if you did you would not identify with it.

What the Ego Conceals about Itself

Let's firstly describe what it does show you about itself. The Ego must show some part of itself to us otherwise we would question it more and more, so it gives us a trivial view to satisfy the little mind we have let it own. To do this it shows us varying levels that we can tolerate and gives us the impression there is an ideal level to achieve. Our world calls these varying levels a range from a small Ego to a large Ego. A small Ego results in people pleasing and a large Ego is self-focused. The master illusionist is great at what it does but it's not perfect like the Holy Spirit. The Ego will set you off on a search for this ideal level of personality within this range, but it always leads to search and do not find. It has created so many courses to go on, so many books have been channelled with the Ego on how to get what you want and improve yourself. Gym instructors improving your body look, diets improving your health, fashion symbols are everywhere to improve your appearance, psychiatrists to improve your mental well-being and skill enhancement in a multitude of ways are out there for you to try and find your ideal place within this range. There are many times in my life I have shown a large Ego which is false self-inflating, and also have experienced many times where I have been overly humble with a small Ego. Let us now not be so foolish. What we are doing here is far beyond all of this. We are not looking for an ideal image of the self within the Ego system, that's impossible. Trust me I have tried and tried. What we are doing here is no longer identifying with the entire thought system to reveal what we were always looking for, the perfect, peaceful, eternal, all loving being within. *It's quite funny actually, we try every day to improve and become a "perfect person", but removing the "person" means you were already "perfect"!* The Ego created the world as a distractive device as a veil over the truth. Why would we look through a veil to find the truth? It cannot be found in form, it's not outside in the world of images. We look through the darkened lens for love, for meaning, for purpose but it's not there. The Ego tells us to come here, you believe you are separated from God, now God will punish you. Come here and look at the world I have made. You lost God, let's make the most of it. What are you looking for, pleasure? We can find it in time and space which I have developed for you where you can find love, friendship, status, success, money, power, and you can have belongings. You can have it with me, not with God. There will be some challenges but with lots of efforts it will come in the future. So, we agree, but the child of God: *"is out of his natural environment and does not function well"* (T-7.11.2:2), and *"A Son of God is happy only when he knows he is with God. That is the only environment in which he will not experience strain, because that is where he belongs in which it was created."* (T-7.11.2:5) Believe in the Holy Spirit through Guru-Je and it will disengage you softly and carefully so you can be who you are. Confidence will grow as it shows you this.

Let's now describe what the Ego doesn't show about itself. The belief in the Ego is a death wish. If you allow it to rule you then you will certainly believe you can die. It will even ask you the question, Who created God? The question is a lie posed as a "fair question" from the egoic point of view. It allows you to doubt God, doubt what you are and gives you a free pass to miscreate. This is obviously insane. To question reality is to question meaninglessly. That is why the Holy Spirit never questions; its sole function is to undo the questionable and this leads to certainty. The certain are perfectly calm, because they are not in doubt. They do not raise questions because nothing questionable enters their minds. This holds them in perfect serenity, and this is what they share knowing what they are. The Ego doesn't give answers. Notice it always asks a question, in particular "What are you going to do about this?" is a typical one. If you are aligned to the Holy Spirit you will know there is no "you" here to answer the question, so it is overlooked. Let's see below what Jesus says in the course about the Ego and what it conceals about itself:

> The body is the ego's idol; the belief in sin made flesh and then projected outward. This produces what seems to be a wall of flesh around the mind, keeping it prisoner in a tiny spot of space and time, beholden unto death, and given but an instant in which to sigh and grieve and die in honor of its master. And this unholy instant seems to be life; an instant of despair, a tiny island of dry sand, bereft of water and set uncertainly upon oblivion. Here does the Son of God stop briefly by, to offer his devotion to death's idols and then pass on. And here he is more dead than living. Yet it is also here he makes his choice again between idolatry and love. Here it is given him to choose to spend this instant paying tribute to the body, or let himself be given freedom from it. Here he can accept the holy instant, offered him to replace the unholy one he chose before. And here can he learn relationships are his salvation, and not his doom. (T-20.6.11:1)

Jesus is quite graphic here. He doesn't want to sugar coat the situation we are in and the teacher we have chosen to live by. He describes this with all of the love of Heaven in such an honest way. If we align with the Ego this is what our life is seemed to be, an instant of despair. After all we make such close connections with everything and everyone and then they all die, and sadness, misery and depression take over. Not to mention that fear embedded within us all of death where the Ego's God ends our personhood. The only release from this is to know it's all a lie and you're not the person who is "living" or "dying". How can we experience some good times and some bad times when the reality of what you are is eternal love? You think you are alive? Being this "person" is blocking your real existence, it's limiting the unlimited. As we give all relationships, objects, situations, and our beliefs away to the Holy Spirit we feel an assurance of being taken care of by the Voice of God. Who else is there to take care of you but the one that created you?

Attraction to Pain – Confusing Pain & Pleasure

Why should the body be anything to you? Certainly what it is made of is not precious. And just as certainly it has no feeling. It transmits to you the feelings that you want. Like any communication medium the body receives and sends the messages that it is given. It has no feeling for them. All of the feeling with which they are invested is given by the sender and the receiver. The ego and the Holy Spirit both recognize this, and both also recognize that here the sender and receiver are the same. The Holy Spirit tells you this with joy. The ego hides it, for it would keep you unaware of it. Who would send messages of hatred and attack if he but understood he sends them to himself? Who would accuse, make guilty and condemn himself? The ego's messages are always sent away from you, in the belief that for your message of attack and guilt will someone other than yourself suffer. And even if you suffer, yet someone else will suffer more. The great deceiver recognizes that this is not so, but as the "enemy" of peace, it urges you to send out all your messages of hate and free yourself. And to convince you this is possible, it bids the body search for pain in attack upon another, calling it pleasure and offering it to you as freedom from attack. (T-19.8.6:1)

I've used this passage before in the body section to discuss the body being a neutral device, but I wanted to bring it back in here for the other important message. The Ego knows the fact that the other "people" and yourself are the same being. The Holy Son of God. It's completely insane to shout, insult, fight, argue, attack or blame the other, as the other is you underneath the veil of forgetfulness. But the way this arrangement has designed the world is for us to be attracted to the whole Ego system. Confusing pain with pleasure. Pleasure is of the body and joy is inward. Unconsciously we are attracted to pain, sin, fear, guilt and suffering. Like a moth to the flame. When I was affiliated with the Ego in my 20s it was quite satisfying to dislike others who appeared to have a problem with me, and to watch them go through problems in their life the Ego would give me the feeling of "they deserve it" – this is completely ridiculous and makes no sense at all as they are you appearing as a different form. Every time I chose to agree with the Ego's thought system, I would block the release of fear and instead absorb it, leaving me with a feeling of vulnerability and open to being attacked by these others who apparently disliked me. After all, if I believed I can attack them or be elevated for their sufferings, then I believe I can be attacked and can suffer as well. We must remember the Ego system isn't the problem here, it's the belief in the Ego. The Ego can do whatever it likes to me in this world but I'm the Holy Son of God and I can step back from it and just watch it as a lie. It's not evil, it's not sinful, it's not wicked – it's just a lie. You don't want to try to analyze your Ego. The Ego enjoys that, although at the start this is the tendency as you learn to understand it. The best thing to do is watch it with Guru-Je holding your hand until you become more unattached to it. You also don't want to try to obliterate the Ego, that makes it real. It will fade away to nothing with Jesus's assistance. You just need to know that you chose the wrong teacher and now you are choosing again, and you choose the right teacher, the Holy Spirit. Let's have a look at what Jesus says about the Ego in the course with my explanation below.

All things work together for good. There are no exceptions except in the ego's judgment. The ego exerts maximal vigilance about what it permits into awareness, and this is not the way a balanced mind holds together. The ego is thrown further off balance because it keeps its primary motivation from your awareness and raises control rather than sanity to predominance. The ego has every reason to do this, according to the thought system which gave rise to it and which it serves. Sane judgment would inevitably judge against the ego and must be obliterated by the ego in the interest of its self-preservation.

A major source of the ego's off-balanced state is its lack of discrimination between the body and the thoughts of God. Thoughts of God are unacceptable to the ego, because they clearly point to the nonexistence of the ego itself. The ego therefore either distorts them or refuses to accept them. It cannot, however, make them cease to be. It therefore tries to conceal not only "unacceptable" body impulses, but also the thoughts of God, because both are threatening to it. Being concerned primarily with its own preservation in the face of threat, the ego perceives them as the same. By perceiving them as the same, the ego attempts to save itself from being swept away, as it would surely be in the presence of knowledge. (T-4.6.1:1)

The Ego doesn't accept the ideas that come from God. This is because they always point to the nonexistence of the Ego. The Ego twists these thoughts or makes it so you cannot hear them – however, it cannot end God's Voice. The Ego is only ever concerned with its own protection, so it muddles unacceptable desires of the body that threaten it and also hides the thoughts of God. The Ego knows it will be brushed away in the presence of the knowledge of spirit.

Any thought system that confuses God and the body must be insane. Yet this confusion is essential to the ego, which judges only in terms of threat or non-threat to itself. In one sense the ego's fear of God is at least logical, since the idea of Him does dispel the ego. But fear of the body, with which the ego identifies so closely, makes no sense at all.

The body is the ego's home by its own election. It is the only identification with which the ego feels safe, since the body's vulnerability is its own best argument that you cannot be of God. This is the belief that the ego sponsors eagerly. Yet the ego hates the body, because it cannot accept it as good enough to be its home. Here is where the mind becomes actually dazed. Being told by the ego that it is really part of the body and that the body is its protector, the mind is also told that the body cannot protect it. Therefore, the mind asks, "Where can I go for protection?" To which the ego replies, "Turn to me." The mind, and not without cause, reminds the ego that it has itself insisted that it is identified with the body, so there is no point in turning to it for protection. The ego has no real answer to this because there is none, but it does have a typical solution. It obliterates the question from the mind's awareness. Once out of awareness the question can and does produce uneasiness, but it cannot be answered because it cannot be asked.

This is the question that must be asked: "Where can I go for protection?" "Seek and ye shall find" does not mean that you should seek blindly and desperately for something you would not recognize. Meaningful seeking is consciously undertaken, consciously organized and consciously directed. The goal must be formulated clearly and kept in mind. Learning and wanting to learn are inseparable. You learn best when you believe what you are trying to learn is of value to you. However, not everything you may want to learn has lasting value. Indeed, many of the things you want to learn may be chosen because their value will not last. (T-4.6.1:3)

The Ego is terrified of the Body and of God since both feel threatening to it. The whole idea of God rejects the Ego, so reasonably it would feel in danger by God. The Ego chooses the body as its home. It feels safe in the body because of the body's vulnerability. Its logic is that the body is vulnerable, so therefore it cannot be of God. On the other hand, the Ego hates the body because it's not considered good enough to be its home. Our mind is confused by this. The mind is told by the Ego that it is really a part of the body and is protected by the body. Although the mind is also told that the body cannot defend the mind. So, the mind asks, "Where can I find protection?" The Ego says it will protect the mind, but the mind knows that the Ego is of the body and cannot offer protection. The mind realizes that it has nowhere to go. Since the Ego cannot provide a resolution, it eliminates the question from the mind's consciousness. Now it cannot be asked and therefore never answered. We must keep the question and always continue to ask, "Where is my protection?" This will lead you to God. The Ego will want to consume you with meaningless busyness. It likes to occupy you with ongoing issues that don't have solutions and is one of the Ego's best tricks. We must always ask ourselves the purpose of everything we do.

It is reasonable to ask how the mind could ever have made the ego. In fact, it is the best question you could ask. There is, however, no point in giving an answer in terms of the past because the past does not matter, and history would not exist if the same errors were not being repeated in the present. Abstract thought applies to knowledge because knowledge is completely impersonal, and examples are irrelevant to its understanding. Perception, however, is always specific, and therefore quite concrete. (T-4.3.1:1)

The Ego will pose the question, how could the mind ever have made the Ego? The Ego will demand many answers that this course does not give. It does not recognize as questions the mere form of a question to which the answer is impossible. The Ego may ask, "How did the impossible occur?" and may ask this in many forms. Yet there is no answer, only an experience. We should seek only this and do not let theology delay us. To ask the question you must still believe it has happened and to answer the question makes the error real. Ken Wapnick says it's like being asked, "When did you stop beating your wife?" There's no way to answer it without getting into a lot of trouble. The way the question is framed it can't be answered without incriminating yourself. The question is really a statement, that masquerades as a question. The question is framed to answer this statement: I believe the Ego happened and now I want you to tell me how, why and who's responsible. If I answer the question, I would be reinforcing your statement. Jesus is also saying here, why are you asking who made the Ego when you are choosing it over and over again. All our history is the separation from God played out in different forms or events over and over again because we haven't forgiven ourselves.

Everyone makes an ego or a self for himself, which is subject to enormous variation because of its instability. He also makes an ego for everyone else he perceives, which is equally variable. Their interaction is a process that alters both, because they were not made by or with the unalterable. It is important to realize that this alteration can and does occur as readily when the interaction takes place in the mind as when it involves physical interaction. There could be no better example that the ego is only an idea and not a fact.

Your own state of mind is a good example of how the ego was made. When you threw knowledge away it is as if you never had it. This is so apparent that one need only recognize it to see that it does happen. If this occurs in the present, why is it surprising that it occurred in the past? Surprise is a reasonable response to the unfamiliar, though hardly to something that occurs with such persistence. But do not forget that the mind need not work that way, even though it does work that way now.

Think of the love of animals for their offspring, and the need they feel to protect them. That is because they regard them as part of themselves. No one dismisses something he considers part of

*himself. You react to your ego much as God does to his creations...
with love, protection and charity. Your reactions to the self you
made are not surprising. In fact, they resemble in many ways how
you will one day react to your real creations, which are as timeless
as you are. The question is not how you respond to the ego, but
what you believe you are. Belief is an ego function, and as long
as your origin is open to belief you are regarding it from an ego
viewpoint. When teaching is no longer necessary you will merely
know God. Belief that there is another way of perceiving is the
loftiest idea of which ego thinking is capable. That is because it
contains a hint of recognition that the ego is not the self.*

*Undermining the ego's thought system must be perceived as
painful, even though this is anything but true. Babies scream in
rage if you take away a knife or scissors, although they may well
harm themselves if you do not. In this sense you are still a baby.
You have no sense of real self-preservation and are likely to decide
that you need precisely what would hurt you most. Yet whether or
not you recognize it now, you have agreed to cooperate in the effort
to become both harmless and helpful, attributes that go together.
Your attitudes even toward this are necessarily conflicted, because
all attitudes are ego-based. This will not last. Be patient a while
and remember that the outcome is as certain as God.* (T-4.3.2:1)

Everyone makes an Ego for themselves, and we build one in
our minds for everyone else too. Egos are not physical objects
we can touch. They are concepts we hold about ourselves. This
is not about how you respond to your Ego, though, it's about
what you believe you are. You are not your Ego, you are not
your thoughts about what you think you are. All your beliefs
you have about yourself are not your real self. Because you
made your Ego, it's not going to be easy to challenge its beliefs.
Sometimes it will be agonizing because we think without our
personality we won't exist. That's not true; we are actually
stripping away what we are not to reveal the most magnificent

creation there is. This stripping away may feel like your world is falling apart, when really it's all falling into place. My little baby girl was once playing with a battery that fell out of the remote. She seemed to bond with it, attach to it, like its shape and was about to put it in her mouth. I reached out for the battery, and she screamed and cried with all of her might. There were tears running down her face despite it still being in her hand. She was unaware of the arduous path facing her if she chose to do what she wanted. The same with us. We are little children unaware of the grueling, strenuous path ahead if we keep identifying with the Ego, and like a child grows up and acquires knowledge and grows out of wanting to put batteries in their mouth we also grow out of playing with the Ego's toys as we follow the course. The Holy Spirit undoes the Ego very gently, to give you a happy dream that merges back to an awakened self in bliss. This will all feel like a dream when we awaken, and it will disappear in an instant. Follow the course sincerely, listen to your guide. It knows you better than you do because it's the memory of what you are.

The Ego & Sacrifice

Only those who have a real and lasting sense of abundance can be truly charitable. This is obvious when you consider what is involved. To the ego, to give anything implies that you will have to do without it. When you associate giving with sacrifice, you give only because you believe that you are somehow getting something better and can therefore do without the thing you give. "Giving to get" is an inescapable law of the ego, which always evaluates itself in relation to other egos. It is therefore continually preoccupied with the belief in scarcity that gave rise to it. Its whole perception of other egos as real is only an attempt to convince itself that it is real. "Self-esteem" is always vulnerable to stress, a term which refers to any perceived threat to the ego's existence.

The ego literally lives by comparisons. Equality is beyond its grasp, and charity becomes impossible. The ego never gives out of abundance, because it was made as a substitute for it. That is why the concept of "getting" arose in the ego's thought system. Appetites are "getting" mechanisms, representing the ego's need to confirm itself. This is as true of body appetites as it is of the so-called "higher ego needs." Body appetites are not physical in origin. The ego regards the body as its home, and tries to satisfy itself through the body. But the idea that this is possible is a decision of the mind, which has become completely confused about what is really possible. (T-4.3.6:1)

Another Ego dynamic is it gives in order to get. It believes in scarcity, lacking and inadequacy. It will bargain to try to improve itself. In true giving, as God gives, there is never a feeling of being taken advantage of or manipulated. Your deepest desire is to extend God's love and be truly helpful. The Ego's plan for helpfulness would be to get something else from another body. It does not matter if this getting seems emotional, psychological, or physical. Reciprocity is the Ego's basic rule for existence. The world of separation was based on the lie of scarcity, needs and exchange. This world of the past, seen as if it were the present, is the misperception of time that the Holy Spirit corrects. The Ego also lives by comparisons, which is completely insane as there is only one of us here, so how can the holy child of God compare with itself? What you give to another you give to yourself, but this doesn't mean you give everything you have away to everyone else because you do not know what is best for them or you. You do not understand your (or their) past, present and future. Instead, we give the responsibility of ownership, maintenance and give away our relationships/ possessions to Guruji or Jesus to manage. They are omnipresent and know what is best for us. This is the peace that arrives on this journey, the fact that we actually don't have to do anything, it's all taken care of for us.

The Ego is Completely Isolated

The ego believes it is completely on its own, which is merely another way of describing how it thinks it originated. This is such a fearful state that it can only turn to other egos and try to unite with them in a feeble attempt at identification or attack them in an equally feeble show of strength. It is not free, however, to open the premise to question, because the premise is its foundation. The ego is the mind's belief that it is completely on its own. The ego's ceaseless attempts to gain the spirit's acknowledgment and thus establish its own existence are useless. Spirit in its knowledge is unaware of the ego. It does not attack it; it merely cannot conceive of it at all. While the ego is equally unaware of spirit, it does perceive itself as being rejected by something greater than itself. This is why self-esteem in ego terms must be delusional. The creations of God do not create myths, although creative effort can be turned to mythology. It can do so, however, only under one condition: what it makes is then no longer creative. Myths are entirely perceptual, and so ambiguous in form and characteristically good-and-evil in nature that the most benevolent of them is not without fearful connotations. (T-4.3.8:1)

The Ego is lonely, it's isolated, it does not want to share. It might try to have other people as friends or form relationships but only to recognize what it is or to blame, judge, condemn and compare in an unconvincing show of strength. There is really only one of us, a one child of God, but there is never any loneliness associated with this due to the nature of the being. It extends into eternity and its creations are one with itself. I love to be alone now but this is very different to being alone when I was Ego centered. Now I enjoy being alone, to go inward and be with my fullness, with the unconditional love, with the warmth, joy and harmony where I know I am fully taken care of. This is not loneliness which is deserted, homeless and abandoned; it is the realization you are whole and complete just the way you are as this being. When I was Ego centered, I was my own God, I ruled my own world. All of us are like this if we believe we are this person. You can't turn to another and say you are more egotistical than me. You either believe you are this individual or not. I had so many friends, a large family, expensive belongings, good health, a fantastic social life, enough money as my parents were comfortable, a large family home and loving parents. With the Ego I felt so independent and strong but reflecting back I was weak because at the center of it I was very vulnerable and exposed. Weak in the sense that others had the power to affect my peace of mind at their will. For instance, being popular supplies our lacks. When that popularity is threatened, we feel deflated as we have a reliance on the popularity to make us happy. In that sense I was a slave. The cunning Ego doesn't want the suffering to last too long otherwise you will look to God for a solution, so it throws you another bone to play with. Maybe this time it will be a good-looking person entering your life, or a job promotion – another temporary distraction technique to keep you focused outward, so you don't look inward. I was empty of full love and only had selected love. If you were a Hindu I loved you a bit more, if you had similar tastes I respected you more, if you supported my team, or lived in my area or shared my interests without threatening my position I loved you more than the rest. Love was not all encompassing like it is now with Guruji and Jesus.

People I didn't know were frightening as I was closed off. With the Holy Spirit I'm open and fearless. When I meet a complete stranger now it's a glorious opportunity to be with myself and see what my mind is telling me about itself. Before I identified with the Holy Spirit people I did know were distorted projections of the truth where I moved between liking and disliking states. As the sayings go, distance make the heart grow fonder and everyone is good in small doses. I was entangled with family politics, exhausting friendship maintenance, and relationships with people as a way of getting away from it all. An example of this is having a group of friends who love to drink whisky, where alcohol was used as an escape from it all. Another example is a group of friends who meet just to talk about others as a venting process. Of course, we know now that drinking excessively to escape from something that doesn't really exist is making a problem out of nothing, and voicing anger or frustration of others repeatably isn't releasing the cause of the issue, but instead reinforcing the destructive nature of the Ego. I now know it's because I chose the wrong teacher, because from the moment I chose the Holy Spirit my life fell into place.

The Idea of not returning Home

You have been convinced that duality is better than the return to God. You are only against the *idea* of not returning. The Ego likes the idea of returning. Why? So, it can make it difficult. As it's an idea. How sneaky this puff of nothingness is. Very clever. That's why the Holy Spirit reminds you that you are already there. This is why we must go through our concepts of understanding. At the start of the course, we go through that initially as it's a course but then we move from that into experience. Like a ride at a fun fair, where your legs press your back onto the wall and the trap floor releases, when the floor goes you won't need the course anymore. You won't need anything as you have your experience keeping you afloat and that ends your doubts. Seek that experience, not your conceptual understandings. You can't know joy, you can only experience it. You can't perform a few miracles and expect it. You need to do it consistently every moment possible, and it will be your experience all the time. Why go joyless when you can bring it in immediately?

Change your mind about the world

The Ego presents the world with many problems, and because we think we are the effect of it, that it's just happening around us separately from us, it also proposes another way to focus on the outside dream and not find yourself inside. It creates "causes or charities" to join with so we can have the feeling of trying to help the world. For instance, charities for heart disease, research for cancer, help for elderly people, abused children and abused animals, clothing charities, adoption of children, wildlife foundations, alcohol and drug abuse, anorexia and bulimia support, art funds, religious charities, Comic Relief, coronavirus charities, diabetes foundations – I could honestly write so many more as there could well be millions. They all appear to touch our hearts in many different ways. We can feel guilty for not giving/participating or also feel guilty for having a life away from it. As soon as we affiliate with one we identify with it and reject the rest. It's a situation where you cannot win, a situation of the Ego. They have all been designed by the Ego; if you want to fix the world in these ways it's like you are chasing a Ghost. They will never be fixed here, because the root cause of them isn't here; it's the separated mind projecting out the pain from believing the disassociation from God. You can't fix it by looking at it with Ego perception, it was designed that way. *Seek not to change the world, seek to change your mind about the world* (T-21.1.1:5). The Ego creates so many forms of pain from this one pain within our mind and the perception is so blinding we can't see through it unless the Holy Spirit gives us a clear perception which is obtained through forgiveness. When Guruji first communicated this to me I was originally offended. I felt like those people out there are really suffering and need my help. But as we go deeper within, we understand that it's a projection of terror, pain and fear of the very instant we chose to leave God. It's a reenactment of openly choosing to leave eternal love. All of these forms are not of God, so cannot have any reality to it. Only God's reality is true. This reminds me of a conversation I had with a colleague from work who said he was an atheist. He said he doesn't believe in a God who creates so much pain and suffering, evil and sin, attack and disease, abuse and degradation. I looked at him and nodded in agreement because this is very much in line with the course. God didn't create any of that, in fact he doesn't even know what it is. I gave money for years to charities believing I was a good citizen and helping those who needed it; 20 years on these organizations are still here. Conspiracy theories around this take you on another detour if we believe that these diseases have already been cured. The thought around this is cures don't make profits for the large pharmaceuticals, problems that need fixing do, so they don't push out the cure. This leads us to want to fight for a cause, for our liberty and for the truth. But the truth is conspiracy theories are another form of distraction device, to keep you looking outward for a "real" answer. We are staring right at the magician's trick, he has us firmly focused while he weaves illusions to search for the truth and protest for it in the world as an injustice. We miss the fact that we are already protesting inside the mind, against our true reality by choosing to be a character here in this dream.

Ego creates Mysteries to look outwards

The Ego also uses other ways to distract you. It loves to create mysteries here so we look outwards for explanations. UFOs, paranormal activity, crop circles. Mysteries provide a breeding ground for the imagination which is the domain of the Ego. A feeling that there is something else greater out there to our world, that feeling is right, but it's inside not out there in these forms. For me, when I was a child I used to be scared of the paranormal like most children and that fear was both frightening but interesting at the same time. Fear through having no control over it, and ghosts being evil in nature. Interesting because somehow it meant there was more to what I see out there. Again none of this is designed to look to the inner being so was a distraction mechanism of the Ego.

The Ego creates a Chaotic Environment

The Ego also creates a Chaotic nature to ensure there is never a unified theory of the universe. If there was a unified theory in its thought system, then leaving it would be simple. One theory is of evolution that biological populations evolve through genetic changes. Another is ice covered the oceans 3 billion years ago and protected organic compounds allowing key reactions to happen began the universe. Another is life began at submarine hydrothermal vents in deep sea mixing molecules together for critical reactions. Another is lightning may have created the first spark to give life. There are many to cause great confusion in our search. If you want the real truth, study the course and you will remember what you are, how you got here and how to get back. In fact, you're already there and never left. In our tiny mad idea of "playing by ourself" God himself didn't acknowledge anything except the idea of perfect oneness, holding perfect oneness for us with him. You're still there, but you have entered into a nightmare state of illusion. While you have travelled only in dreams, God and Child, who are always one, have continued as they always did and always will. Remember to not be fooled and be impressed by new discoveries or theories about life because they're diversion techniques.

Taming vs Overlooking the Ego

A big issue the Ego likes to create when we take the course seriously is to get us embroiled in taming the Ego instead of overlooking it as a lie. When I became a vegetarian, I was fixing a problem I was suffering from, meat addiction. Like a cocaine addict I needed it as much as possible to satisfy. At the time this was before the course, but I was connected to Guruji and he transitioned me off the dependence of it. I was freer, but it's not until now that I realize, he was using the Ego to loosen the hold. The final cutting off from all suffering came with the course when he showed me being a vegetarian is also of the Ego. To be truly free I must transcend time and that only happens with aligning with spirit who is outside of time. What I was doing when coming off the meat was taming the Ego. As Vegetarianism, Veganism and pescatarians are all forms created by the Ego I was simply shifting forms for a bit more comfort but releasing the entire idea completely was true freedom. At the start of the course you can definitely feel like you're taming the Ego, as you feel like you're sacrificing something. In fact, as you go deeper, how can you sacrifice what is not there? The real meaning of sacrifice and deprivation is "the cost of believing in illusions". Guru-Je asks only for you to give up the belief in a made-up world. We must give Him not sacrifice, but the whole concept of sacrifice. So, a couple of points to take here are the Holy Spirit uses the Ego symbols of the world to undo it, and secondly taming by renunciation is not what we are doing here. We are not renouncing the world, because then the world will appear as a huge sacrifice. We are changing our mind about the world which leads to complete peace. At this moment I'm mainly a vegetarian, but to be open to the lie on both sides of the coin I'll pick up some meat now and then at parties to demonstrate to myself that it has no power to change the peace and love my creator has with me.

All laws of Nutrition are of the Ego / Jesus on Magic

This next section is likely to surprise everyone who reads it. I used it in Chapter 6, The Body, to discuss the body's sickness briefly, but let's go deeper into this on nutrition.

Section from *A Course in Miracles*, Workbook Lesson 76 – I am under no laws but God's.

We have observed before how many senseless things have seemed to you to be salvation. Each has imprisoned you with laws as senseless as itself. You are not bound by them. Yet to understand that this is so, you must first realize salvation lies not there. While you would seek for it in things that have no meaning, you bind yourself to laws that make no sense. Thus do you seek to prove salvation is where it is not.

Today we will be glad you cannot prove it. For if you could, you would forever seek salvation where it is not, and never find it. The idea for today tells you once again how simple is salvation. Look for it where it waits for you, and there it will be found. Look nowhere else, for it is nowhere else.

Think of the freedom in the recognition that you are not bound by all the strange and twisted laws you have set up to save you. You really think that you would starve unless you have stacks of green paper strips and piles of metal discs. You really think a small round pellet or some fluid pushed into your veins through a sharpened needle will ward off disease and death. You really think you are alone unless another body is with you.

It is insanity that thinks these things. You call them laws, and put them under different names in a long catalogue of rituals that have no use and serve no purpose. You think you must obey the "laws" of medicine, of economics and of health. Protect the body, and you will be saved.

These are not laws, but madness. The body is endangered by the mind that hurts itself. The body suffers just in order that the mind will fail to see it is the victim of itself. The body's suffering is a mask the mind holds up to hide what really suffers. It would not understand it is its own enemy; that it attacks itself and wants to die. It is from this your "laws" would save the body. It is for this you think you are a body. (W-P1.76.1:1)

I really admire Jesus's honesty in the course. He is opening up all of our beliefs that limit our freedom. Let's discuss nutrition.

All laws of nutrition are of the Ego. Food is an idea; in this world it is an unreal effect from an unreal cause. The Ego creates categories such as high calorie/low calorie, high fiber/low fiber, organic/nonorganic, good nutrition/bad nutrition. Where the Holy Spirit would accept, the Ego Analyzes. The gratitude of wholeness comes only through acceptance, but the Ego wants to break down into smaller parts to separate out. The Ego believes that power, understanding, and truth lie in separation; it's obsessed that separation is salvation, by breaking it into small, disconnected parts, without meaning.

These categories are what Jesus calls Magic. Through our selective memory which is based on judgments and preferences we determine if something has high or low nutrition. As we research the world's nutritional ideas, we become a Master of it. The one who becomes a master of magic is a magician. To the sleeping mind magic appears to work, this is why over the years I have met hundreds of people at various gyms who have different ideas on nutrition that seems to work for them. Whether it's eating organic foods or having a low-calorie diet, or a high protein intake these are all forms of magic. The so-called effects of these forms are here to distract us from the mind. If I'm dieting, I think I dislike my body. Actually, I don't dislike the body. I really dislike what I think I have become by believing I'm separate from God. Our mind is so conditioned it's a huge shift in perception from ego thinking to spirit thinking. Herbal remedies and supplements all seem to work alongside medical procedures that have been claimed to be very successful. It's looking for solutions outside of you to try to heal you, but this is quite surprising if you think about it, you're the entire universe and beyond, created by the most magnificent creator and you need magic to heal you? You've put the problem outside of you, then you say there's the problem over there, it's my diet (a form you have selected), then you focus on your limited methods that sometimes work and sometimes don't, that sometimes work for others but not for everyone else and say great this works for me now. All the while you have set this up to ignore the real problem which is the lack you feel inside being without God's eternal fullness. These forms of healing are about feeling better about the body which leads to elevated temporary happiness. However, these are attempts to achieve peace through mastery of fear. I have been on many strict diets, and when I do this, I am saying I can come to some mastery through my skills, abilities and past testing. Jesus teaches us the only thing that will succeed always is the mastery of love. Diets and belief in nutrition are rearranging fear to bring happiness. Sciences are based on that thought, changing this and that to get to a credible hypothesis. Whether it's herbal science, acupuncture, massage therapy, these are all designed to make you briefly happy by using methods outside of you. It's funny how whenever I'm finished with a massage they always give me a voucher for the next visit, it's built in to not last – surely you would want more longevity to your peace?

Only Self-Realization will be the cure. The world is causeless as is any dream that has been dreamt. It's been created by the Ego not God. If we believe in this world the effects will be real to us. If we follow the Holy Spirit the effects are gone. We need to pull ourselves within away from all past testing and towards the spiritual awakening that shows us the separation never happened. In life we go through many experiments, fasting, vegetarianism, herbal solutions, and other systems. As we go deeper inwards, we start to see that the cause is the mind and there aren't causes and effects in the world. This takes a lot of practice to not make exceptions with that; it has been part of my journey as well. I asked Guruji, "If I eat deep fried food, chocolate, cakes, and fizzy drinks I'm obviously going to get fat and feel unhealthy, so what are you saying here?"

It's a belief that if you eat too much fatty foods you will get fat. There seems to be plenty of evidence in the world for that. And then there are those that have a high metabolism and eat lots and do not get fat. How can some get fat and others not? It's because nothing in this world is a fact. All nutritional information is subjective. Getting fat is a judgment made from the past, the past is nonexistent. Then there's the direct link to the future as "getting" fat which is hypothetical theory – the future is nonexistent. You have completely missed the present in between. Being in the present you will be guided by the Holy Spirit on what to eat and drink for nutritional purposes, but tell me this, what is fat but a completely made-up concept? Since the day you entered this world, you have been sent millions of signals from the outside world telling you what attractiveness and good health is. The models, the posters, the "fatless pinups" that are all over the TV and shopping malls have conditioned your mind to suffer to feel lack in you and to do something about it. What is strength, the 6-foot male model with a six-pack on the beach, or the overweight, topless guy who doesn't care what you think of him? The first is vulnerable to keeping the image up, exhausted from the maintenance and supplies it lacks with a temporary solution. But being fat or not is not the point here. If we go into that territory, we make the body very real. The point is to give the whole idea of body shape and nutrition to Guru-Je who will heal it so we don't feel lack in us to shape the body, but use the body for what it is meant for: the Holy Spirit to communicate through. Food choices need to come from within not the outside. When I go into a supermarket, I like to scan the food and feel what the inner self wants. The mind on the other hand has tormented me many times by choosing what gave me pleasure before and wanting it again, and that's when overeating occurs. The sense of not enough and needing more by eating more than the body wants. Realizing you are not that body entity that needs more is crucial here.

The Holy Spirit works with the mind with what it believes. From a relative perspective, diet, fresh air and exercise seem to be helpful. I continue to feed my family with what comes in my belief as healthy foods and drink. But over the years I have worked on my thoughts and emotions. The best thing to do is ask what do I really want here? The answer is healing and happiness. Only when the mind is substantially trained does the law of nutrition fade away. Like a fire walker not getting feet burned on coal. The appetites fall away. The cravings and needs, and food will become like a part of the set. But your inner guide is very practical. Guru-Je will direct you to that peace. Remember whatever you fight you give strength to, and whatever you resist, will persist. Surrender and you will be joyful. In my life script Food was a very big deal. My entire family were big eaters, very passionate about it and this is why it's an area which I struggled with most. Jesus worked with my script and didn't pull all of the foods I wanted from under my nose right away; it was done slowly and gently. The Holy Spirit also paired me up with my Wife who is actually a very well-disciplined eater. Content with the simplest of foods and has very little cravings. I have learnt much from being around her every day. This leads me nicely onto Special Relationships.

Special Relationships

You cannot love parts of reality and understand what love means. If you would love unlike to God, Who knows no special love, how can you understand it? To believe that special relationships, with special love, can offer you salvation is the belief that separation is salvation. For it is the complete equality of the Atonement in which salvation lies. How can you decide that special aspects of the Sonship can give you more than others? The past has taught you this. Yet the holy instant teaches you it is not so.

Because of guilt, all special relationships have elements of fear in them. This is why they shift and change so frequently. They are not based on changeless love alone. And love, where fear has entered, cannot be depended on because it is not perfect. In His function as Interpreter of what you made, the Holy Spirit uses special relationships, which you have chosen to support the ego, as learning experiences that point to truth. Under His teaching, every relationship becomes a lesson in love.

The Holy Spirit knows no one is special. Yet He also perceives that you have made special relationships, which He would purify and not let you destroy. However unholy the reason you made them may be, He can translate them into holiness by removing as much fear as you will let Him.

You can place any relationship under His care and be sure that it will not result in pain, if you offer Him your willingness to have it serve no need but His. All the guilt in it arises from your use of it. All the love from His. Do not, then, be afraid to let go your imagined needs, which would destroy the relationship. Your only need is His.

Any relationship you would substitute for another has not been offered to the Holy Spirit for His use. There is no substitute for love. If you would attempt to substitute one aspect of love for another, you have placed less value on one and more on the other. You have not only separated them, but you have also judged against both. Yet you had judged against yourself first, or you would never have imagined that you needed your brothers as they were not. Unless you had seen yourself as without love, you could not have judged them so like you in lack.

The ego's use of relationships is so fragmented that it frequently goes even farther; one part of one aspect suits its purposes, while it prefers different parts of another aspect. Thus does it assemble reality to its own capricious liking, offering for your seeking a picture whose likeness does not exist. For there is nothing in Heaven or earth that it resembles, and so, however much you seek for its reality, you cannot find it because it is not real.

Everyone on earth has formed special relationships, and although this is not so in Heaven, the Holy Spirit knows how to bring a touch *of Heaven to them here. In the holy instant no one is special, for your personal needs intrude on no one to make your brothers seem different. Without the values from the past, you would see them all the same and like yourself. Nor would you see any separation between yourself and them. In the holy instant, you see in each relationship what it will be when you perceive only the present.*

God knows you now. He remembers nothing, having always known you exactly as He knows you now. The holy instant reflects His knowing by bringing all perception out of the past, thus removing the frame of reference you have built by which to judge your brothers. Once this is gone, the Holy Spirit substitutes His frame of reference for it. His frame of reference is simply God. The Holy Spirit's timelessness lies only here. For in the holy instant, free of the past, you see that love is in you, and you have no need to look without and snatch love guiltily from where you thought it was.

All your relationships are blessed in the holy instant, because the blessing is not limited. In the holy instant the Sonship gains as one, and united in your blessing it becomes one to you. The meaning of love is the meaning God gave to it. Give to it any meaning apart from His, and it is impossible to understand it. God loves every brother as He loves you; neither less nor more. He needs them all equally, and so do you. In time, you have been told to offer miracles as I direct, and let the Holy Spirit bring to you those who are seeking you. Yet in the holy instant you unite directly with God, and all your brothers join in Christ. Those who are joined in Christ are in no way separate. For Christ is the Self the Sonship shares, as God shares His Self with Christ. (T-15.5.3:1)

Special relationships are all those you choose to have here. Lovers, friends, cousins, uncles/aunties, grandparents, siblings, parents, life partners, children and grandchildren. Before we entered this life as this character, we already at a higher level decided our script, who will be in it and what part they will play. Your parents didn't have you as their child, you have collectively chosen to be their child in this lifetime as well as for them to be your parents. In every relationship each of the persons involved is both persons, because everything is an externalization of the mind's thoughts. When we heal relationships through forgiveness and see everyone as sharing the same purpose, we are uniting our own split minds. Healing isn't my relationship with you, from body to body, because your body and mine are both projections of my mind. What is healed is my relationship with myself. In healing my relationships with the people in my life (especially close family), I am bringing back the projections of my divided self, recognizing no division and they are the same. This elevates my mind's unity, which is the greatest healing. Relationships are so crucial as they are the only way of being in contact with the actual problem. When *A Course in Miracles* talks about special and holy relationships with people what this means is there is only one **special relationship** we have, which is with the Ego, and only one **holy relationship** we have, which is with Jesus, the Holy Spirit, Guruji or your preferred symbol. We project either one onto the people in our lives. So, it is not our relationships with others that have to be healed, as they are simply classrooms in which we learn where the real healing needs to be; which is our error in choosing the Ego. The truth here, that really opened my mind, was **we do not require special relationships with people. There are no people. This is the reality, the most important factor.** If you look at people, they are always changing, their image, their wrinkles, their hair loss, their grey hairs, their thoughts always changing, because the body persona is a process not a fixed entity. Ken Wapnick says people are like puppets; as the puppeteer tells the puppet what to say and do, similarly the mind is telling people what to say and do at every moment. Puppets don't need to forgive other puppets; the play has been scripted so all problems here are designed to conceal the only problem we have. Forgiving people for what they appear to do here (forgiveness to destroy), on the superficial surface, only reinforces the make-believe reality in a puppet's play when it's just a scripted play after all. Ken says our relationships which we think are real because we think we are bodies are only projections; the dark parts of our special relationship with the part of the self we call the Ego, which identifies with separation and hatred. However, what has happened here is forgetfulness has masked over the truth, we have forgotten we have a mind, and so thankfully we have these relationships to perceive in the body to remind us of the mind which is where the problem and the answer are. The parent-child relationship is one most filled with guilt and suffering because it is the closest in form to our relationship with God. The parent-child relationship pours out so many issues we have with the Ego's version of God that we have believed. The millions of apparent tiny and large issues on the surface which we see are not the real problem, we have believed the secret dream which is the core of suffering. When my toddler throws her food on the floor every other day, cries to not go to bed or has tantrums on random occasions she's actually the angel in my life showing me the problem in my mind to be released and forgiven. You could say she's not the angel we thought she was! We need to experience that conflict with the authorities in our lives starting with our parents so it can be recognized for what it really is and released. As children we then grow up and become parents or elder mature figures for others. So, the special relationship is played out until we bring it back to the only special relationship there is, which is our reliance on the Ego. When we are finally aware of this all relationships are healed, as the one problem has been brought to the one solution. Handing off all Special relationships to the Holy Spirit or Guru-Je is the beginning of the Holy relationship which is where our gentle lessons begin.

With Special relationships there is special love and special hate. Love is now selective and not all encompassing so it's actually not really love. Special hate is where we feel it's acceptable to project hate and anger onto someone; special love tends to be a relationship in which we believe that only a special person can meet our needs. Though they look quite different in form both are two sides of the same coin; they say that our separation from God can be solved through an external relationship. So when we are talking about special relationships (with a person, landscape, an object) we are externalizing an inward condition. It must be healed within the mind. In *A Course in Miracles*, Jesus tells us that special relationships can be transformed into holy relationships. That is, relationships in which oneness is revealed rather than hidden. So, it's not about giving things up or becoming celibate; rather it is about learning how to perceive correctly.

My wife and I have been married for many years now and what keeps us in love is we don't look to each other to wholly complete us. It would be completely unrealistic and unloving to expect another "person" to make you whole. If you can't love yourself first, you cannot possibly love another person. True love is a communion between two beings (which are part of the whole one being), felt inwards deeply that it can't really be expressed in words. Happiness resonates within us and we don't "need" each other to complete us and make us happy but the other is an equal companion with no powerplay or domination. This removes fear and insecurity. If we completely relied only on each other then we would be placing our fulfilment on an external factor which will never lead you to true peace and happiness as it becomes a replacement for God's eternal love rather than a part of it. Our relationship was given over to Guruji from the start even if I didn't fully know it back then. I have done many miracles from Guruji who prompted it through her, and I also practice the course on her. In potential arguments I practiced "in my defenselessness my safety lies" and enjoy serving her as my creator's child. One of the best lessons I learnt from this relationship is the way I behave with you is coming from the way I behaved with God.

Eckhart Tolle once said:

What is conventionally called "love" is an ego strategy to avoid surrender. You are looking to someone to give you that which can only come to you in the state of surrender. The ego uses that person as a substitute to avoid having to surrender. The Spanish language is the most honest in that respect. It uses the same verb te quiero for "I love you" and "I want you", to the ego loving and wanting are the same, whereas true love has no wanting, no desire to possess or for your partner to change. The ego singles someone out and makes them special. It uses that person to cover up the constant underlying feeling of discontent of "not enough" of anger and hate, which are closely related. These are facets of an underlying deep-seated feeling in human beings that is inseparable from the egoic state.

I have special relationships with my parents, siblings, wider family, my small child and my wife's parents and family as well. The Ego tells me to make them the most important special people in my life, that they are to be loved more than others and treated better than others. Jesus is saying if we do that, we exclude the rest of love, and love is whole not selective. Now on the surface this obviously seems to create a huge dilemma as this is how the world operates. But Jesus isn't saying to love your family less and love others more; he is talking about the attachment to these special parts of the mind. There's a piece of mind here, another there that projects out characters in the dream world. When we attach and feel inseparable from these other parts of the mind, we reject the others and so are not unified. This is honestly one of the Ego's chief obstacles to eternity. Have you ever spoken to people who want to be united with their loved ones when they "die", and God who created them, sustains them and loves them unconditionally is not their first choice or even considered? If we look at our loved ones closely, they are the being inside, they are not the body that you want them to be; the body is something they can have and have had many times. So, what are you exactly attached to? If you see these relationships through the eyes of the Ego you will value them over God. They will be your excuse to come back here again and again. Maybe next time I'm the parent or the sister – it doesn't really matter it's the Ego recycling of the separated mind using these images of characters we are attached to. If we choose the Holy Spirit, we don't see our loved ones as these small individuals, we begin to see them as a part of the whole, that death cannot separate us, and that in God we all are awake. In this world, on the surface there isn't much that changes, we still prioritize our special relationships, but you are much more open to others who are not in your relationships bubble. If an elderly person is struggling you may assist them, as you can see, they are you in a different form. If other people's children are crying you will reach out and support rather than just think of your own children and as that's not your problem. The people outside these special relationships hold much more value to you than they did before. Also, within your own relationships bubble you are not concerned about different opinions or choices, and with the Holy Spirit you are much more attune to "what is this telling me about my mind to be forgiven" so you are very thankful to them for showing you the issues in your mind to be released. You are not scared of being separated from them one day, because you know it's a lie, in life their bodies may appear to separate from you from a variety of circumstances; moving homes, relocating to another country. In some belief systems changing religion or sexual orientation can cause detachment, going to prison and death is the final separation. None of these are real; with forgiveness the Holy Spirit unites you through the miracle and shifts your perception. All memories I have of my dad that passed away are of the Ego. They are nonexistent and painful because I cannot relive them, change them, or enjoy them again. Because they are painful, they are not of God. If I wanted to be with my dad which version would it be, the 20-year-old version, maybe 40 or 65? The fact there's different versions demonstrate the unreality of him. It's his being inside that I loved, and I am with him inside of God right now because the separation never happened.

Ego Amplifies Problems

Let's move away from special relationships and into further ways the Ego creates issues. The Ego loves to amplify problems in order to make itself real. I was recently in a tricky situation at work where it felt like a colleague was doing work that I usually do and asking me for my work in order for them to do their own version and give it to the same people. The Ego was very vicious; it implied, what are you going to do about this, he's taking over your work? The Ego amplified the situation in my mind to the point where fear was trying to lose my whole purpose of work. I immediately kept my mind still and stepped back as the observer. I could see the waves of cloud-like thoughts circulating Akash's mind, viciously trying to make Akash attack the person, then when I didn't respond, it tried to make me defend the position and protect Akash's Ego. Again, I became the watcher, not identifying with these thoughts as they are not me, and read out my forgiveness in my mind with Guru-Je. I stepped away from the laptop for a few minutes and could see that the colleague was chasing me for my work in an e-mail. Suddenly a higher thought came in; I could tell the difference because it was gentle, calm and all-knowing so didn't need to be vicious. It said to call an executive board member and gave me their name. I asked what to say and it replied to gain their support to not share your work and tell the colleague you can't share it. It was incredible; usually this board member is away and not available, but when I messaged her, I got an instant response and she said she was available now for a quick call. This is the synchronicity of consciousness, linking us all together. She immediately agreed with me and I closed the situation off with an e-mail.

The Ego reinforces its reality through conditioning the Mind

I was recently playing with my daughter who is a toddler, and she loves fairy tales, animations, nursery rhyme video songs and cartoon books. We were watching the TV together, a nursery rhyme called five little ducks. As I was watching it Guru-Je gave me very interesting thoughts. From the day we are born we are conditioned with illusions. If we see cartoons, moving pictures and animal characters on the screen, we interpret them as made up, fictitious and unreal because when we go to the park and see ducks the scene isn't like that and the ducks are not like that either. You can also not use all five senses with the screen, but you can smell and touch in the park with ducks. These animations on TV and books reinforce the reality of this world and is an Ego trick; from birth we are conditioned. By seeing something obviously unreal (the animations) the other appears to be more real (our world), but more real isn't true existence. The Ego creates "not real" so we can say our world is real and I'm a real person in it. My toddler grows up and then she likes make-believe play with all sorts of things, preparing us make-believe tea, biscuits and meals in her children's kitchen. Now she knows it's make-believe as she knows what's in our kitchen, but by having what isn't real the other feels a lot more real. This continues into our teens and adulthood with movies and TV shows. We have something to say like, "Oh that's just a movie, it was so terrifying but it's scripted with made-up characters and scenes," and gives the feeling I have my life to come back to after. You won't think you're dreaming if you can see dreams in other fantasies outside as the dreams are over there, never over here!

Then there's the education system. We have been educated to be separate from everyone else. You have never been taught the oneness of your being with all of existence. This is why it is alien to you. Instead we are taught: competition, survival of the fittest, pass your exams and you will make it, become an entrepreneur and you're successful. The only faith we have is found in religions but religions divide us into categories and it's only universal spirituality that brings us all together to love everyone as ourselves.

The Sky is one illusion we should look at. But what is the Sky? Like everything else here, it has no reality. Let's investigate this:

Since the day we were born into this world, the Sky has always been there. The Analogy is the Sky is the unrestricted consciousness and clouds are thoughts of mental ideas or concepts. When we are deeply identified with our mental ideas, the unlimited consciousness becomes cloudy and the best comparison to inner vastness or stillness is the clear Sky. I find this fascinating as the Sky isn't there, it's a word to describe an empty space. Travelling upwards you can't locate it as it has no beginning or end. Its existence isn't the same as objects in our experience such as a car or a chair. You can never pinpoint when you are inside it or when you have made contact with it. There's somehow the joining of both the enormity of outer space with the appearance of a blue dome which has sunlight. This illusion that something is there is what we call the Sky. In spirituality, the sky often referenced as it is equivalent to the inner emptiness or the fullness of ourselves.

Watching the Ego's Play (by detaching from the Character) / Being Vigilant

I remember when I first started the course, I found it difficult to actually understand what this Ego thought system really was. One morning I was flicking through channels on the TV and could see that a movie which I liked was coming on called *300*, so I recorded it to watch for later. I remember watching the movie with Guruji, and there was a moment when I went to join with him where he is, and I stepped back from my thoughts. I could see the movie, the feelings arising from it and the thoughts creating the feelings. I looked at the thoughts and although I didn't affiliate with the thoughts, I knew what they were. They were attack thoughts for the bad guys in the movie and supportive thoughts for the victims. In the movie the tyrant was Xerxes and the hero was Leonidas. Xerxes was going to destroy all of Sparta and Leonidas led 300 Spartans to war against him.I was watching the movie but also watching these thoughts go by (notice I said these thoughts, not my thoughts). If I didn't step back I would be engulfed in the drama. The Queen that was assaulted while the King was at war gave rise to strong victim thoughts. She then killed Theron who had assaulted her so the feeling was revenge and justice. Then came all the war scenes of good guys beating the bad guys and the thoughts wanted the good guys to kill and destroy the bad guys and win the battle. Guruji showed me something very powerful here, that I must monitor my thoughts in everyday life and not identify with them. As you identify with them you identify with the Ego, and it will then try to pull you in and amplify the situation. It does all of this to make itself real. We have spent all of our lives identifying with these thoughts and believing they are us, but they aren't. How are you able to step back and watch the thoughts if they are you? We can watch our reactions, see how quickly we choose up sides. Even though we know it's all made up in a movie we still get upset when the good guy gets hurt and bad guy wins. We also feel great when the bad guy loses. I tried this with everything I watched on TV, when I read the newspaper, watching sports etc. to practice it. You know that you're making it when you can laugh at everything, not in a mocking way, but because it's all the same. What we've made serious we've made up. Just watch yourself without judgment or anger. The world we are in is just as unreal as the movie. In fact it's a moving picture of images, streams, sensations, feelings and thought. Of course, the Hero of your dream is always you and there will be plenty of villains. But remember Leonidas and Xerxes are characters, the real actors are Gerard Butler and Rodrigo Santoro who walk off the stage to live their lives after. Gerard and Rodrigo never really think they're Leonidas and Xerxes, it's an act! Similarly, Akash is the character, played by the being inside. This being has played many characters before and this is the one to experience now. This brings us nicely onto what Jesus says in Chapter 6 of the course, Be Vigilant Only for God and His Kingdom.

Be Vigilant Only for God and His Kingdom

This is a major step toward fundamental change. Yet it still has an aspect of thought reversal, since it implies that there is something you must be vigilant against. It has advanced far from the first lesson, which is merely the beginning of the thought reversal, and also from the second, which is essentially the identification of what is more desirable. This step, which follows from the second as the second follows from the first, emphasizes the dichotomy between the desirable and the undesirable. It therefore makes the ultimate choice inevitable.

While the first step seems to increase conflict and the second may still entail conflict to some extent, this step calls for consistent vigilance against it. I have already told you that you can be as vigilant against the ego as for it. This lesson teaches not only that you can be, but that you must be. It does not concern itself with order of difficulty, but with clear-cut priority for vigilance. This lesson is unequivocal in that it teaches there must be no exceptions, although it does not deny that the temptation to make exceptions will occur. Here, then, your consistency is called on despite chaos. Yet chaos and consistency cannot coexist for long, since they are mutually exclusive. As long as you must be vigilant against anything, however, you are not recognizing this mutual exclusiveness, and still believe that you can choose either one. By teaching what to choose, the Holy Spirit will ultimately teach you that you need not choose at all. This will finally liberate your mind from choice, and direct it towards creation within the Kingdom.

Choosing through the Holy Spirit will lead you to the Kingdom. You create by your true being, but what you are you must learn to remember. The way to remember it is inherent in the third step, which brings together the lessons implied in the others, and goes beyond them towards real integration. If you allow yourself to have in your mind only what God put there, you are acknowledging your mind as God created it. Therefore, you are accepting it as it is. Since it is whole, you are teaching peace because you believe in it. The final step will still be taken for you by God, but by the third step the Holy Spirit has prepared you for God. He is getting you ready for the translation of having into being by the very nature of the steps you must take with Him.

You learn first that having rests on giving, and not on getting. Next you learn that you learn what you teach, and that you want to learn peace. This is the condition for identifying with the Kingdom, since it is the condition of the Kingdom. You have believed that you are without the Kingdom, and have therefore excluded yourself from it in your belief. It is therefore essential to teach you that you must be included, and that the belief that you are not is the only thing that you must exclude.

The third step is thus one of protection for your mind, allowing you to identify only with the center, where God placed the altar to Himself. Altars are beliefs, but God and His creations are beyond belief because they are beyond question. The Voice for God speaks only for belief beyond question, which is the preparation for being *without question. As long as belief in God and His Kingdom is assailed by any doubts in your mind, His perfect accomplishment is not apparent to you. This is why you must be vigilant on God's behalf. The ego speaks against His creation, and therefore engenders doubt. You cannot go beyond belief until you believe fully.*

To teach the whole Sonship without exception demonstrates that you perceive its wholeness, and have learned that it is one. Now you must be vigilant to hold its oneness in your mind because, if you let doubt enter, you will lose awareness of its wholeness and will be unable to teach it. The wholeness of the Kingdom does not depend on your perception, but your awareness of its wholeness does. It is only your awareness that needs protection, since being cannot be assailed. Yet a real sense of being cannot be yours while you are doubtful of what you are. This is why vigilance is essential. Doubts about being must not enter your mind, or you cannot know what you are with certainty. Certainty is of God for you. Vigilance is not necessary for truth, but it is necessary against illusions.

Truth is without illusions and therefore within the Kingdom. Everything outside the Kingdom is illusion. When you threw truth away you saw yourself as if you were without it. By making another kingdom that you valued, you did not keep only the Kingdom of God in your mind, and thus placed part of your mind outside it. What you made has imprisoned your will and given you a sick mind that must be healed. Your vigilance against this sickness is the way to heal it. Once your mind is healed it radiates health, and thereby teaches healing. This establishes you as a teacher who teaches like me. Vigilance was required of me as much as of you, and those who choose to teach the same thing must be in agreement about what they believe.

The third step, then, is a statement of what you want to believe, and entails a willingness to relinquish everything else. The Holy Spirit will enable you to take this step, if you follow Him. Your vigilance is the sign that you want Him to guide you. Vigilance does require effort, but only until you learn that effort itself is unnecessary.

You have exerted great effort to preserve what you made because it was not true. Therefore, you must now turn your effort against it. Only this can cancel out the need for effort and call upon the being which you both have and are. This recognition is wholly without effort since it is already true and needs no protection. It is in the perfect safety of God. Therefore, inclusion is total and creation is without limit. (T-6.9.3:1)

Being vigilant for only the kingdom was a tricky lesson at the start. In the course Jesus walks us through how vigilant we already are for the Ego's kingdom. Every time someone offends us, helps us or flatters us we are the first to protect/sustain/ agree with our self-image made. If someone says I look so handsome and slim, the Ego wants me to identify with it and find happiness in that, but how if that is not me? We do this every moment of our lives. Sustaining our self-image at work, with friends, with family relationships. We are very vigilant in the world for upholding our image by dressing the body, learning new skills, making more money, increasing our status and raising our popularity; they need constant vigilance for protection. Attacking back at others who insult what we think is us and making an ally of those who compliment us. We are very, very vigilant for our made-up self, our self-created kingdom. We are also very vigilant for other people's Egos. He is like that, she is like this, but how vigilant are we of our real self? Before I started the course it was zero. Thankfully the wholeness of what we are doesn't need protection as it will always be no matter what we believe. But our awareness of this kingdom must be protected to hold its presence in our mind and not let doubt enter – We are protecting the awareness of our wholeness, so we don't become doubtful of what we are. Therefore, vigilance is vital. Vigilance is not necessary for truth, but it is necessary against illusions. If we are not vigilant, we can be influenced by the Ego's lies. This will lead to a loss of our awareness of the Kingdom of God, that will never mean the kingdom of God is lost, because that's impossible as we are the kingdom, but like clouds come in and hide the light we will not experience it. You are being vigilant on God's behalf. We know that the Ego has no reality, but if you identify with it you will believe it and become uncertain of the totality of what you are. We are already included in the Kingdom of God's one love; it is only the belief that we are not in the kingdom that we must exclude from our minds. Another way to put this is God's Kingdom cannot be a kingdom without its child, you are the child that makes it into a kingdom. We cannot even faintly understand how loved we are by our creator; it's far beyond our concepts of love. Like little children are fully dependent on their parents, we must become fully dependent on the Holy Spirit. Then when you wake up from the dream you merge back with God and are fully dependent on it – whose care is the most loving nirvana, bliss, paradise there forever is. One question I had here was, if the Ego is nothing, wouldn't being vigilant for it make it real? The answer I received was Vigilance is of the Ego, but as we are seemingly here, this perceptual realm is of the Ego, so we need to be alert not to identify with the Ego, so vigilance can be used as a purpose for attentiveness by the Holy Spirit. At the start we believe we can still choose the Ego or the Holy Spirit, but as we teach what to choose, the Holy Spirit will ultimately teach us that you need not choose at all. This will finally liberate our mind from choice, and direct it towards creation within the Kingdom and vigilance is no longer needed.

The Authority Problem

Let's move onto The Authority Problem and how the Ego causes illusions around this.

The authority problem. This is "the root of all evil." Every symptom the ego makes involves a contradiction in terms, because the mind is split between the ego and the Holy Spirit, so that whatever the ego makes is incomplete and contradictory. This untenable position is the result of the authority problem which, because it accepts the one inconceivable thought as its premise, can produce only ideas that are inconceivable.

The issue of authority is really a question of authorship. When you have an authority problem, it is always because you believe you are the author of yourself and project your delusion onto others. You then perceive the situation as one in which others are literally fighting you for your authorship. This is the fundamental error of all those who believe they have usurped the power of God. This belief is very frightening to them, but hardly troubles God. He is, however, eager to undo it, not to punish His children, but only because He knows that it makes them unhappy. God's creations are given their true Authorship, but you prefer to be anonymous when you choose to separate yourself from your Author. Being uncertain of your true Authorship, you believe that your creation was anonymous. This leaves you in a position where it sounds meaningful to believe that you created yourself. The dispute over authorship has left such uncertainty in your mind that it may even doubt whether you really exist at all.

Only those who give over all desire to reject can know that their own rejection is impossible. You have not usurped the power of God, but you have lost it. Fortunately, to lose something does not mean that it has gone. It merely means that you do not remember where it is. Its existence does not depend on your ability to identify it, or even to place it. It is possible to look on reality without judgment and merely know that it is there.

Peace is a natural heritage of spirit. Everyone is free to refuse to accept his inheritance, but he is not free to establish what his inheritance is. The problem everyone must decide is the fundamental question of authorship. All fear comes ultimately, and sometimes by way of very devious routes, from the denial of Authorship. The offense is never to God, but only to those who deny Him. To deny

His Authorship is to deny yourself the reason for your peace, so that you see yourself only in segments. This strange perception is the authority problem. (T-3.6.7:2)

Throughout my life I have had so many conflicts with authoritative figures. They come in many forms but Jesus here is so clear, there's only one problem and the Ego weaves it into so many different forms we can't see the wood from the trees. Jesus is telling us very clearly that we have a problem with the fact that God is our Author, and we have attempted to author ourselves, to also usurp (or take) God's power, throne, place or purpose. This attempt, which we believed seriously attacked or killed God, is the hidden source of all guilt. In the separation, we refused His role as Creator and tried to be creator in His place. We tried to create our own self and even to create God. However, we only achieved in making a self-image, the Ego. Now we believe we can change ourselves (a form of creating ourselves) by changing our image. The outcome is an authority problem as we project this belief (in self-creation) onto another person, which leads us to fear that he or she can take our function of self-creation away from us and can use creative power over us or can alter us against our will. This is all illusion. Since we did not author ourselves, we have no power over what we are, nor do others. We have not seized God's power and have no origin for guilt.

In my life the authorities have caused me so much distress, through parents telling me what to do, teachers grading me unfairly, the government imposing restrictions/new taxes, senior members at work grading my performance, elder family members imposing their traditions on me, a hospital telling me I can't stay the night when my baby was born due to COVID-19 regulations, the bank taking down my interest on savings or increasing the interest on loans, the police stopping my car for no real reason and car parking wardens fining me for the two minutes I was in the shops. Would we ever have thought that these are all varying projections from the one problem where we believed the Ego that we attacked God, tried to take his throne, thus believing we created ourselves (an individual self-concept) and we felt so guilty for doing this that we pushed it out of our awareness and onto all of these forms, so they are the ones to blame not me for my choice of apparently leaving God. When I read this first, I was astonished, and it was even quite unbelievable, but trust me if you forgive your authoritative figures for what they have not done and yourself for choosing the wrong teacher in the Ego – the Holy Spirit will give you the experience that confirms to you that this metaphysical situation is true. For the first 30 years of my life, I blamed them all for all the reasons above, and it made me lonely, miserable and it kept happening to me in different forms because I didn't forgive and release it for what it was. When I understood the authority problem all these situations started to lose their effects on me, as I was really just forgiving myself for what I have not done. None of this was really happening to me, just appearing that way as the separation from God never occurred for any of this insanity to be true.

Recently my manager and his boss wanted to have a review with me about some work that they needed to understand from me. It was classic authority problem scenario territory for me: they were telling me what to do, how to do it, undermining my decisions and the Ego wanted to viciously attack them with anger and defend my image. I stepped back, read the forgiveness quickly in my mind, kept quiet for 10 seconds, held Guruji's hand in my mind and let him talk through me. What he said was very clear to everyone, it was respectful, it was technical, it was accurate, and it was calm and playful. It gave them the feeling they were in control on the surface but also the assurance that my skills are made for this work and there's no one else who knows it better. We laughed, they became friendly, supportive, and it was not at all a big deal like my Ego made for hours before the meeting. That all happened on the surface. Deep within Guruji had made the correction, he connected us with our unified mind, allowed me to see them as the Child of God for a holy encounter and to give them their place in the Kingdom. Always remember that everyone is looking for himself and for the power and glory he thinks he has lost. When you are with anyone you have another opportunity to find them; your power and glory are in him because they are yours.

Being Egotistical isn't "Having an Ego", the Ego is the entire Personality

The attributes of the Ego must be known so it can be forgiven and reversed; so the light of God can shine through the Ego's illusions for it to disappear. I wanted to return to an important point that most people get confused about – the Ego is not "being egotistical"; it's an entire thought system from one of two choices. A conversation I recently had with a close friend feels so relevant to this point. We will call him Adam. Adam and I have another friend in common who we will call Tom. Adam says to me, "Akash, we are both very spiritual and some people confuse religion with spirituality. I hope you don't mind me saying but Tom has a lot of Ego. Every time I tell him about my day and the things I have achieved he has another answer which makes what I have done seem smaller. I was telling him how when I was growing up, we had a wealthy upbringing and had maids and gardeners to assist us, which Tom replied he had a few big houses with cars and cleaners to help every day. I then mentioned we had so many parties and events all on my dad's one salary, to which Tom said my dad was in one of the highest posts in India, a well-revered man. I was also saying to him that when I arrived in the UK I had nothing at all and with my wife had to build all of this with my hard work and efforts (Adam was clearly well off now as well as in his childhood)."

The conversation continued on and on as I quietly heard Adam talk about Tom as if he were any different. This is what I mean when I say it is not common knowledge to know what you are up against when you join the Ego thought system. Clearly Adam believes being egotistical is unspiritual whilst at the same time the Ego has a very tight hold of his thoughts and beliefs making Adam feel as if he is a person, with a life, with a history, with memories that make him who he is today and tricking Adam into believing Tom has Ego and he does not. *The Ego is not the same as being egotistical.* Even if you are less egotistical you are still identified with the Ego. You have to completely disidentify with it and reestablish the connection with the Holy Spirit. This is an illusion. All past arises from the present moment and then evaporates back into consciousness. This is happening all the time. We are walking through space-time choosing what we want to see. Gathering our past and trying to be a person who is individualized and special. This person is constantly changing as new experiences arise and beliefs change thus changing the perception. The truth is you are not the individual. I am not Akash being spiritual, I am the spiritual being beyond Akash's thoughts. Like the Sky is always above, the clouds come in and appear to block it, thoughts arise and appear to block the being which is infinite.

The Ego makes us afraid and so reliant on having our thoughts that we feel life cannot exist without them. It's right to some respect, the person (i.e., Akash) cannot be in the material world without thoughts but as you can see when you close your thoughts you are still here. In fact, here still (in mind). Something is here watching the stillness, something so grand and peaceful is allowing this body to exist and be alive (that's if we call this "living", surely living is everlasting).

The Ego – The Master Illusionist
Like a magician keeps your vision fixed on what he/she wants

while the trick is being completed out of sight, the Ego is deceiving. I'd like to share some experiences of this deception:

Individual experience:

Akash supports a North London Soccer Team called Tottenham Hotspurs. This team has an arch-rival in North London called Arsenal. All rivalry is of the Ego, because it reaffirms separation between us, it divides us and puts us into categories which are opposing, for conflict. If we agree to this conflict in our mind, we establish this division and confirm to be a false self-personality. Akash's friends support Arsenal, and when Akash had his first child these friends very strongly communicated their viewpoints that Akash's child should support Arsenal. Additionally, Akash wanted his child to support Tottenham as his life script has been set up for this conflict. Now on the surface Akash perceives this as an attack on his Ego, a feeling of loss, then unhappiness through disappointment follows, and what the Ego always does when it feels attacked is to attack or defend its position in an attempt to fill its inadequacies. The first feeling which builds up is outrage and anger towards the people, to want to verbally tell them, "No, it's my child she supports my team," etc. This anger is created because the Ego thought system is the embodiment of fear, feels lack in itself, so needs things outside of the body to supply its shortfalls. This issue, on the superficial surface, can be analyzed much closely; if you ignore it, however, you have fallen for the trick. Let's go deeper:

Firstly, from football competition, Akash felt a loss of his child to a rival, let's go inward further.

Secondly, this loss is actually how I felt when I chose to give up everything in existence, that is total love, wholeness and eternity with our creator; to be this little person.

Finally, we go deeper into the stillness, this giving up is a lie, we haven't lost who we are and our eternal relationship with the supreme is always there, it's changeless.

This is the master illusionist at work. Telling me that the problem is out there, it's my friends who have made me upset and angry, and it's their fault. Keeping my sight firmly focused on trivial concepts like Tottenham and Arsenal, and missing the trick. I was looking at the form and missing the content. Tottenham, Arsenal and my child supporting them wasn't the problem. The real problem is the secret dream (which isn't really a problem, it's a belief that there is a problem), the fact that I chose the Ego and I chose it over my real creator God. When I chose the Ego I absorbed enormous guilt, because I chose to be my own God, to take over the real God and take his place at the throne to make my own world where I am the center of it. We all did this at the separation. This guilt was so difficult for the mind that we had to become mindless to move on, so we as the child of God projected out a universe, and at this point in time Akash is perceiving this separation in Tottenham, Arsenal and losing his child to a rival. I have put the problem there, nobody else has done that. As I have chosen the Ego I put it there so I can conveniently attack other parts of myself outside of me and blame them so that the egoic separated mind lives on in space-time. Listen closely, I have two choices. I can choose the Ego and attack back, get angry, prove my point and get what I want; or I can choose again and choose the Universal mind (Holy Spirit) to unify Akash with all of his loved ones and undo the Ego with joy, love and peace. I chose the latter and to this day have never felt so peaceful. I said to myself, "I'm innocent, whole and spirit, all is forgiven, and all is released. The separation from God never occurred and I'm in perfect oneness with God eternally. I chose the wrong teacher. I now choose the right teacher. I choose the Universal Mind and Guru-Je." Physically I did not really say very much to the people and kept it minimal with other bodies but as we know there is no gap between body and mind, and Guru-Je had adjusted space-time so my experience was unified with the friends who support Arsenal and had minimal conflict and much peace. This forgiveness meant that space-time was shortened and we were closer to being at one with our creator (although I know from outside of time, I was already with God). If I had chosen the Ego and went into heavy debates, arguments and if I joined the battleground of the physical world, then this separation would have come up in my life again in another form and I would have had the opportunity again to forgive or keep the dream going. I now am so grateful to the Arsenal friends who are givers of the gift. They showed me the problems hidden in the mind. All that was needed from me was to give the darkness to the Holy Spirit so it can bring it into the light to evaporate.

Collective experience:

In March 2020 COVID-19 had reached the UK's shores and a huge pandemic was upon the nation and the world. As the year progressed many people died, lots were infected, and many suffered through isolation and mental illness as lockdowns emerged. What also emerged was the egoic battleground, two sides appearing of different opinion and conflicting arguments. The first were the government who say the disease was created in China through bats and now the world has an outbreak of disease which will kill us if we don't find a vaccine or cure. This side led so many television and media messages for restrictions, lockdowns and fear-based ruling. The other side were the believers that the entire virus was orchestrated by the government in order to kill people, reduce the population and bring further layers of control to take people's freedoms away. Similar to Arsenal-Tottenham, there are always two sides seemingly conflicting. The Ego magician is there to keep your vision firmly rooted on the battleground so you would not see the real problem, the secret dream held closely hidden within the mind. There are not lots of problems, only one. The problem isn't in the virus. The problem was in the separated mind and it was projected onto the world as a virus of separation. All of the daily virus updates, through the main media channels of communication and the undercover messaging describing the virus as a hoax were there for only one reason, to keep me firmly mindless so that I can see the problem outside in the world to keep me busy so it's not my fault it's out there, and to think that's where the problem is. This is the illusion. The truth is there is no gap between body and mind. If the body suffers it's because the mind suffers. The mind is suffering because it chose the wrong teacher and believes it is separate from its creator, the child of God chose uniqueness over oneness with God. It chose to be an "I", a "person" over universal equality. It then couldn't deal with the guilt as God only gives love unconditionally in an unlimited way, so it suffered immensely and needs to escape the pain by making a world where the problem sits outside, and we can be ignorant to it. We can appear as innocent (when really we *are* innocent, there's no need to *appear* to be) as the problem just happens to us when really it's coming from us. Guru-Je the universal mind immediately gave me the interpretation that something was wrong here. The Ego created the other side to make it out the disease is the hoax so you still stay mindless and fight on one side, but the Holy Spirit knows all. It's perfect and gave me the interpretation that this entire world is a hoax, and the secret dream is buried deep within the mind and must be forgiven. So I played my part and forgave myself for choosing the Ego over God, and being a decision-making mind I chose again. I chose Guru-Je the Universal mind. I said to myself, "I'm innocent, whole and spirit, all is forgiven, and all is released. The separation from God never occurred and I'm in perfect oneness with God eternally. I chose the wrong teacher I now choose the right teacher. I choose Guruji and Jesus." What came next was simply incredible. All fear of the virus was removed. I was just not worried or concerned for my life at all. I respectfully listened to all of the accounts of death and experiences from the other parts of me and didn't feed them the spiritual talk as we are all in different stages of our journey, like if I make two points on a circle neither are ahead or behind the other. They had their experiences because that was for them to have. I felt fearless, full of all the gentle strength from the Universal mind and didn't really enter into heavy debates of either side of the battleground. I forgave lots of times as I could see separation in so many ways, from loss of loved ones, missing family members separated due to health, lockdowns separating all of us from being together and even us being separated from holidays abroad. It was all forgiven and released, and peace of mind filled me every day. I was awake.

Discovering what I am With Guru-Je & Living life with ACIM

– Being the Better Person isn't accepting another's apparent errors and personally trying to be better, how can that be when it's you who has projected the error onto them to see this as outside of you? For Peace, Love & Joy you would overlook what is being acted out by the other Person and release the error with your Better Being. –

An Egoic Life

The first 30 years of my life I would say I lived a very typical life of a man in this world. Using a metaphor, the script in my play was very much engrossed in Maya, the illusionary world. I really believed I was Akash living in a world with all these different people, objects, images, forms and events. I was much more identified with the Ego than with the Holy Spirit. I had a completely conditioned mind and a personality which I believed was myself. I worked my way up through the education system from nursery, infant, junior, senior schools, college, university, and then professional exams with a career. I had a large friendship group and was extremely social. I grew up in a large wider family with so many uncles, aunties, and cousins. I was born into a Hindu family with both loving parents, until I lost my dad in the same year which I was married at the age of 30. Losing my dad was the trigger to letting God back into my life after seemingly 30 years of living without God. Most of us ARE living without God, with few exceptions of true spiritual masters like Jesus, Guruji, Guru Nanak and Buddha. Let me remind you what living with God is. Just like when a drop of water falls into the ocean and becomes part of it again as the water merges and becomes one with itself, the real "you" is the drop that merges with its source of creation. What I mean by living without God is, can we speak to God directly every second of the day? Can we be completely encompassed with its love, peace and Joy at every moment and create by keeping what we have and extending further and further into eternity? No is the answer as this only happens in the realm of the absolute where only God is. We are not there right now, we are in the realm of the physical, which is a universe governed by Guilt, Fear, and darkness – Created by us. This has not happened to us; we want to be here as delusional as it sounds. We think we are born into this world, with a family, friends, and a "life". Clearly in this "life" we are appearing as separate people, where God is in the sky, in a temple, a church, a mosque, a synagogue outside of us. We have to find God out there, that's if we even believe in God that is. Our bodies are designed to look outwards, our ears listen outwards, our eyes look outwards, our nose smells aromas from outside, our mouth receives tastes from objects outside, our skin feels sensations from the outside world. We actually believe we are in a world as a person separated from God. We give him some time, maybe play some holy songs in the background, visit a holy place now and then, attend religious festivals filled with things to do so we can feel like we have checked in and said hi to God. I prayed to God now and then when I needed something. Sometimes I got what I wanted, other times I did not, and I actually blamed God at times. I was a little child even at 30. Some people remain a little child all their lives and do not outgrow their little toys. We have done this for lifetimes because we protest against our true reality. These little toys include chasing image status, desiring wealth to feel above others or wanting to be poor so we can blame the world for our situation, focusing on physical body appearance and pleasures, chasing false power in careers, feeling lack in yourself if you are not popular and well liked. Even trying to be the hero and save the world from its problems is of the Ego. Once I volunteered to support a homeless shelter at Christmas one year and did three days at a center to assist homeless people. It was early in my spiritual journey but looking back the homeless people were like bodies in my play showing me what is in my mind. So, you can forgive yourself. When I created this script with the Ego I felt homeless, disbanded from the kingdom of God and had projected my guilt from choosing to leave onto this dreamlike stage. The world is an outside projection of an inward condition. The problem here was not poverty, it was that they were unwanted. Love is not about attachment, where we just enjoy each other. Love is free and comes from divine origin. It's an unconditional force alive in us. I wanted to help my brothers who were unwanted. Actually it was an appearance of unwantedness, and underneath the veil of illusion my brothers were there fully taken care of by our creator. Nothing is so blinding as perception of form. They are here so I can choose again and reestablish myself with them as the child of God. The world keeps us so busy all our "life" that we can easily keep God out with activities that are temporary whilst shutting out the eternal peace of the kingdom inside us. Doing our charitable work is not an achievement we put on our CV, it's a beingness, an action of giving and is certainly not "me-ology" of blessing everyone. If we look closer, we will see people are the images we have made. Love them, respect them but there is no need to do charitable work so you can blame others who do not do the charitable work. Do it as a loving expression of what you are. This will only happen wholly when we know what we are.

The Trigger to Find the Truth

As I sat beside dad in the hospital bed with me, I never had a chance to say goodbye, his body was cold, lifeless and still. I was in disbelief that this is how it all ends, and although I was very sad to see Dad go, I could see myself here in the future. A calling from the mind came, a call to come back home where I was loved unconditionally; an unlocking of intensity for self-realization emerged. The funeral was soon upon us and Hindu Rituals bombarded my life. I never knew what many of them were for and I had deep sadness through mourning with the family; we were all lost. It seemed that I was the one with the greatest opportunity ahead. I was newly married and lived reasonably far (90-minute car journey) from the family home so could relatively detach from the circumstances quicker that my siblings and mother who had to deal with the everyday loss at the family home. I had a new married life to jump into and keep me occupied. I immediately jumped into self-realization books written by the great A.C. Bhaktivedanta Swami Prabhupada who wrote the *Bhagavad Gita: As It Is*. At that time reading these materials was like jumping straight into the deep end, and I was not really ready for it. The circumstances around me did not mean I progressed much, but unlike before I was firmly surrendered into God and not rejecting him. As I tried to search and understand these studies I became vegetarian which was quite the opposite to my carnivore nature. I would say this brought peace for me as I had a compulsive desire to eat meat every day and in changing my habits it meant my mouth was not ruling me, but I was freer. Although I am a vegetarian seven years on, I would take Pursah's advice from *The Disappearance of the Universe* by Gary Renard: "As long as you don't make it real. Like anything else, if being vegetarian is done from a place of love and as an expression of love, then it is a beautiful thing, if it's done to make other people wrong for NOT being vegetarian, then it will imprison the mind."

Connecting with Guruji

I wanted to advance spiritually. I was ready to give up my little toys one by one in order to advance, but I needed help, so internally I called for the grace of God to guide me back home. The weekend after my call, my wife's parents invited me to an unusual event, called a Guruji Satsang (a sacred gathering) with a Sangat (followers of a Guru). A Guru is the one who has swum to the shores of enlightenment and come back to bring you with them. At a high level the student has called for his Guru and they connect in the physical world when the time is right. Being Hindu I had been to many Satsangs in my life, but although my body was there for these my mind certainly was not. My mind was focused around playing with my phone and checking sports scores or messaging friends. A Satsang is so beautiful. It's the gathering for the Truth usually from a Satguru for instruction. Now, this Satsang was different, the Guru was not here in form, he had consciously laid the body to rest in a practice called Mahasamadhi. I was intrigued as my wife's mother and my wife described the Guru to me. He fixes all problems, he communicates with you through the Hindu symbol OM which can mean the symbol appears in your food, in your drink or anywhere for you to perceive, he knows all your past-present-future, is aware of your destiny and can change it, he is the incarnation of the master Lord Shiva. I also heard things which made my skeptical mind laugh. You must eat all the food given even if it's too spicy or if you don't like the taste. I remember my wife's mum telling me she once had a hot green chili arrive in her plate and it was a test from the Guru, so she ate it and did not feel the heat. The food blesses you and heals your body. I was suspicious and unconvinced but attended anyway as I needed help. Immediately I was enriched by the atmosphere when I arrived; it was warm, peaceful and the Sangat were loving and kind. The bhajans or hymns were beautiful and there was quiet time also for me to empty my thoughts. This is where I first felt the connection to him. It was like I was finally at home, like all my life of mindless activity was for this moment of connection. It only lasted a few minutes for me, but I knew something special had happened. I didn't find any OMs in my food but it was delicious food. I left not really knowing what will happen next. A few days after, for the first time in my life I developed severe tinnitus which is a constant ear ringing. It must have lasted three weeks, and I felt I had to go inwards for joy as the ear ringing was a hindrance to the outside world. I was reading a book at the time by Deepak Chopra, the spontaneous fulfilment of desire and from his topic of Syncrodestiny and seeing the web of coincidences in our lives. I knew the Guru had arranged this, after all I was fully surrendered to him. Through research I found out that he was clearing my energy blocks so I can listen better to my intuition. Our intuition is like the quiet voice inside, giving you clear, calm guidance. While the inside of your mind can be like a crowded elevator full of people talking it's hard to hear that guidance.

A month had passed, and I was onto reading a handful of recommended spiritual books, maybe five or so arrived into my life; I read the books on weekends and went out for walks to continue reading in my lunch breaks at work. It was slow progress as my workplace became a lot busier. I gained a promotion, but because I was working 12 hours a day I could not find any time to read the books as much I wanted to. I managed to get through half of them when a dramatic change came over me. I was becoming frustrated with this slow progress as work gradually became my second priority and spirituality the first, despite having commitments in a householder life with bills to pay. I called the Guru again in my mind, "Please give me the time to finish these books. I want to progress, I want to come to where you are." I kid you not, the week after I received a letter in the post for two weeks Jury Service. I was over the moon and knew he had organized this for me. I actually only had one case to be involved in and I managed to finish all the material. It was Godsend.

When I returned back to work, I felt that although I gained a promotion I was underpaid, plus I was working so hard my mind was occupied on mindless activity at work for most of the day with nothing really to show for it at the end. It was a blue-chip, shareholder listed IT company and all my output was making shareholders (people who are already wealthy) wealthier. From all the material I had absorbed I felt a shift in consciousness and wanted two things. Firstly, I wanted more money to make financial pressures go away, and secondly to be part of a new company where they help the world and the different parts of myself progress in life. I consulted my senior counsel inside, my Guruji. I remember nothing really much happened over the week, but I did sign up to Not For Profit Industry jobs mails on my phone. The week after, I remember looking through my mails and suddenly to my disbelief there was a job which paid very well, with almost the exact same job specification as what I was already doing. All I needed to find out was what the output of the company was, what was their cause? I called the job agent up and they said it was the UK's largest Not for Profit which focuses on education, teaching and learning for people all over the world, and through its charitable nature helps people to gain education if their life did not allow them the same opportunities as I had been brought up with in the UK. E.g. Students in Syria being displaced from their universities due to war – this company helps them to finish their education. I knew this was the job for me but having worked for so many companies before I was afraid of the recruitment process. The online tests, three rounds of interviews and an assessment center was what I was used to. Frightening and exhausting. I had faith in God and my Guruji, and started the process. There were to be two interviews, which made me smile. I attended the first one and to my surprise all the questions I was asked I had prepared for; it was very smooth. Then the agent calls me back for feedback afterwards and says the second-round interviews have fallen through as the interviewer had important work to do, however, would like to offer me the job. *I was stunned*! I had spent nearly 10 years after graduation going through the painstaking interview process and this one time with Guruji I was handed the job. I felt it was my destiny, or more accurately said it was the Guru changing my destiny by adjusting space-time. *A Course in Miracles* talks about Jesus adjusting space-time to reduce it so you do not need to go through certain problems again after you have forgiven the circumstance. If you are uncomfortable with using Guruji, Jesus, Krishna, or Buddha as symbols of God personified then the course talks of the Holy Spirit or the Universal Mind which I also use when I forgive. All the symbols are the same. They are the Non-Ego part of you, but sometimes it's easier to use an image to make the connection easier; mine was Guru-Je (Guruji & Jesus). That evening I bought a chocolate cake after work to celebrate the new job. I put it in the fridge. When we took it out at dinnertime, I witnessed a Godsend moment. A huge, crystal clear OM on the cake box. This further reestablished my faith and my gratitude poured out to God. I was speechless.

The next day I was bold, brave, and handed in my notice. I had to give three months' notice but with less work to do as I could focus on handover, I was excited to see what the next material was. I had a deep yearning inside to increase my knowledge and go deeper, especially around the metaphysical universe. I finished *The Seven Spiritual Laws* by Deepak Chopra, and then I could feel the big, life-changing pure nondualistic material coming into my awareness. I wanted to study *A Course in Miracles* which Jesus Christ channelled through Helen Schucman over a span of seven years. I downloaded the correct material as I asked Guruji for it. There was so much material to get through with 1,333 pages and also in this there are 365 workbook lessons where you are instructed to do only one lesson a day. There was a lot of commitment required indeed. I researched the best ways to approach the course and found it would be made easier if I read what most course students would agree with as the best introduction to the course, which were four books that put the course into very simple language. The books were written by Gary Renard and they were life changing: *The Disappearance of the Universe, Your Immortal Reality, Love Has Forgotten No One,* and *The Lifetimes When Jesus and Buddha Knew Each Other.*

I clearly had a couple of years ahead of me of studying, but for me it was a hobby. With three months of notice to serve, lots of annual leave to use and much more free time I managed to get through Gary's books as I started my new job. I felt so much more aware of how the universe works, what I am and my relationship with my creator. At first my new role was busy, they needed my help dramatically, but I was fixed on doing my 9am-5pm time only and leaned on Guruji to guide me. He connected me to everyone. For everyone who needed my help there was someone else God had given me to assist me. It was vastly interconnected. I knew a deadline was coming up and then the next day help would arrive with what I needed for that deadline, as the course says, *"you need do nothing,"* (T-18.7,5:3) was so correct. I grew more and more confident with Guru-Je that I used to do little prep for meetings and just turn up and ask him to talk through me. It was amazing what came out to all these senior people. I eventually came to a state now that I'm really just speaking to myself and every conversation is either a call for love or an expression of love. Nothing else. The ones screaming at me, needed my help and love, and the ones being kind to me were showing their love and appreciation. It was beautiful. The trust grew and grew as I handed everything over to Guruji to arrange for me.

When I began the course, it took me two years to complete. I was worried at first how I would find the time to study, but actually Guru-Je had a marvelous plan. It took me 45 minutes to arrive at work and 45 minutes to come home, and this new job was travelling by train so I could sit down and study. He wanted me to study on the train, Monday to Friday for 90 minutes a day. At first, I thought this was a joke, but actually looking back they were absolutely incredible. Guru-Je was so connected to everything he would give me a workbook lesson to read in the morning, then reinforce it by giving me real life examples at my work to use the lesson on, and then I would reread the lesson and go over the day on the way back home. It was as if Jesus was using the people I work with and the situations to teach me the lesson. I was so grateful all the time as I knew I was being handheld.

I am as God created me

Today we continue with the one idea which brings complete salvation; the one statement which makes all forms of temptation powerless; the one thought which renders the ego silent and entirely undone. You are as God created you. The sounds of this world are still, the sights of this world disappear, and all the thoughts that this world ever held are wiped away forever by this one idea. Here is salvation accomplished. Here is sanity restored. True light is strength, and strength is sinlessness. If you remain as God created you, you must be strong and light must be in you. He Who ensured your sinlessness must be the guarantee of strength and light as well. You are as God created you. Darkness cannot obscure the glory of God's Son. You stand in light, strong in the sinlessness in which you were created, and in which you will remain throughout eternity. Today we will again devote the first five minutes of each waking hour to the attempt to feel the truth in you. Begin these times of searching with these words:
I am as God created me. I am His Son eternally.

Now try to reach the Son of God in you. This is the Self that never sinned, nor made an image to replace reality. This is the Self that never left Its home in God to walk the world uncertainly. This is the Self that knows no fear, nor could conceive of loss or suffering or death. Nothing is required of you to reach this goal except to lay all idols and self-images aside; go past the list of attributes, both good and bad, you have ascribed to yourself; and wait in silent expectancy for the truth. God has Himself promised that it will be revealed to all who ask for it. You are asking now. You cannot fail because He cannot fail. If you do not meet the requirement of practicing for the first five minutes of every hour, at least remind yourself hourly:

I am as God created me. I am His Son eternally.

Tell yourself frequently today that you are as God created you. And be sure to respond to anyone who seems to irritate you with these words: You are as God created you. You are His Son eternally.

Make every effort to do the hourly exercises today. Each one you do will be a giant stride toward your release, and a milestone in learning the thought system which this course sets forth. (W-P1.94.1:1)

I recall a time when I was to meet my boss's boss who definitely wanted to show me that he was the boss. This leader has now left the business, but looking back I can definitely see he was there for my lesson learning with Guru-Je. As I entered into his room after his Personal Assistant welcomed me in, I knew he was going to use his false power to get what he wanted. He needed me to write a good note to the board to allow his investment to be agreed. I was firmly focused on Guru-Je, asked him what he would have me say to only be said. I remembered *I am as God created me* from the morning train ride, and he was as God created him, so I was kind and loving not because he was my boss's boss but because my creator created him as well. Guru-Je did not let his feelings be hidden, and spoke through me with power, honesty, humility and sincerity which the boss recognized. Of course, the boss did not admit to taking my advice and he did not thank me for it, but his actions spoke when I found out that he instructed his leadership team members to make the changes to the investment business case which I recommended. Basically, I was marking his work and what Guru-Je said was so accurate that he took it on himself to make the changes. I also wondered how Guru-Je got me in such tricky situations which were so entangled. It was because this was how I was to learn and experience the course in a practical way. Also, to deal with my Karma and undo the mess I created in the first 30 years without God.

More on the New Job with Guru-Je

I remember at work in my end of year review they called Akash trustworthy because he was reliable. Looking much closer at this reliability it had limits imposed which were set by conditions. If Akash was given a demotion in responsibility, an extreme overload of work fixed into his role or given a new boss that was constantly disrespectful suddenly this would change. **Trustworthiness** is really if we **Trust** our Inner Guru which is a holy symbol that connects us to our Higher Self, we will then realize that we are the **Worthiness** ourselves. For us to ignore our worthiness is a demonstration that our attitude isn't worthy.

As my career progressed, I recalled that for the first 12 years of my career I was affiliated with the Ego; I wanted to be successful, rich and powerful and worked in large blue-chip multinational environments. I was brainwashed into a fear-based system, so fearful my leaders would teach me to always be alert of how my personal image is being shown to others, to sign up to presentations, to meet up with other departments and be my own brand at work so when the next job becomes available the other departmental leaders will think of me and hand the job to me. They also taught me the elevator pitch method, which is to always be preplanned to know what to say if you were in an elevator (or a short time alone) with another top leader to leave a good memory of yourself with them. These methods cause such strain on the mind which is constantly ticking and focused on the Ego self-image. It's mentally exhausting as you become entangled within the illusionary hierarchical work system. This is completely in the opposite direction as the unified field where the ego self wants to get what it wants only and misses the interconnectedness of us all. It's important to remember the leaders are the same as you, created by God equally. Why would you be a slave to their opinion of you? This work system's solution is then to go on **Holi-day** when it all becomes too exhausting; what we really want to do is take a break from this tiresome idea of ourself, if we only follow the Divine Self and deny Attack thoughts through Holy Forgiveness then every day becomes a **Holy-Day**. Guru-Je was incredible, he took this all away with my new job. He took it so far away that I was in a state of planning nothing whatsoever ahead of some calls and meetings, and being so open for him to enter and speak accordingly through me.

When I was being trained in the course by my internal Guru, I knew I needed empowering. I thought I needed it to do a better job at work for him but now watching it back from where I am today it was because he wanted me to be empowered so I was disciplined to always be vigilant for the Kingdom of God in my mind and to not identify with Ego thoughts whatsoever at all. He taught me this discipline through a close colleague at work who I had to partner and support. She was a tough person to manage, constantly needing work to help her, always asking questions, inquiring about every little detail. I had to be alert, present and awake to deal with the constant bombardments. Guru-Je was teaching me the same discipline must be done with the mind. I was always three steps ahead of her, completed work before she asked, and if she did not ask for it, I recommended it. The course calls this Miracle-Readiness, be on your toes to forgive instantly. The Kingdom of God is already there but we have let the dark thoughts come in and then we have identified with them, so the kingdom is hidden with a thick veil. Therefore, strict discipline is needed to always be watchful. *"Get dressed for service and keep your lamps burning; be like people waiting for their master to come back from the wedding celebration"* (Luke 12:35-48 Bible.org). What Jesus means here is, by always being alert, the servant cannot rest and put their feet up, so always be watchful to protect the mind from Ego thoughts. The Ego is the thief that takes away your peace, that which limits what is unlimited if you choose to believe it.

Undoing the Ego

After I had completed the course, I knew this was just the start. Jesus and Guruji brought me into this making me feel like I was learning more. Actually I was slowly undoing my Ego which I called Akash. This was not a course to make Akash's life better, make him richer, make him more popular, make him successful, and give him more of life's pleasures. It was a course to show you there is no world out there, it is your Ego belief in Guilt being projected outwards and showing you through images, streams, and sensations what is in your mind. It's a course to bring you back to unconditional, everlasting love. We believed the Ego's lies and accepted the Guilt from being separated from God, from this Guilt comes all the anger, greed, violence, attack, and darkness of this world. The Ego is not the problem, it is the belief in the Ego that is the problem. You believed the Ego to be here, you can unbelieve it to go back. *The Ego is the programmer, and you are seeing the program played out.* It is not a "life", its activities are there to keep you mindless, so you focus on the thousands of happenings here and do not look inside to decide again that you want to be with God in its peace and love forever. You cannot be here and also be in God's

Kingdom, they are diametrically opposed. One wants you dead, the other says you cannot die. One says you need people, things, events, beauty, fame, fortune to be happy; the other says you are Joy and everything so what is there to need? You can only arrive in the Kingdom with no images, no thoughts, no person, and no attachments. When you go to meet the emperor, you wear your finest clothes, you clean your teeth, you put on nice aromas to smell better, you shave or style your hair, you look your best. The same here: you are going back to God, remove the little nothings, no thoughts, no desires, no wishes, empty the blockages and bottlenecks that prevent you from being the perfect eternal fullness that you are. We think when we lose the person, we lose our life. That is not true. When we lose the person, we finally see our true identity, whole, innocent, and complete. We can love unconditionally as we are certain that we are loved unconditionally by our source.

Surrender everything to Guru-Je

After three years of practicing the course on everything in my perception I could sense an urge to have children with my wife. They say children bring you new karma. Karma is action and usually having children creates bad Karma because we get further entangled into the Ego thought system. So, when making the children I surrendered to Guru-Je and said I do not make the children with the Ego for special relationships and worldly success, I make them with the love of God to fulfil what I'm destined to do. I handed the care over to Guru-Je like I handed my career, my home, my bills, my relationships, my body, and life objects also. Remember everything outside of you is temporary, even the children. Look at my dad who vanished off the face of this earth in an instant. Love the children, not specially but wholly and do not rely on their love to make you happy. There's only everlasting love from God and the Guru; you can rely only on that who connects all the pieces of yourself together. Children can be used by the Ego to keep you very busy in mindless pastimes or when given up to the Holy Spirit they can be used as a way to freedom. It's so much fun when it's all been organized for you, it's peaceful and in between their naps on the weekends you can even write a book!

When COVID-19 arrived, we were all told to work from home with immediate effect. Coincidentally this was the year I had my first child, my wife was on maternity leave. Guru-Je organized my work calendar, moving meetings around so I could assist my wife in between meetings and put the baby to bed while she could rest too. I kid you not, I could see my wife struggling and there were so many situations when the meetings were either cancelled or moved forward in the week or even later, which meant I could jump in, support my wife then attend another call when they were both resting. Every day I surrendered and every day I was taken care of. Angels from work arrived who have now left. They came to assist me through challenging times which I could not have done without them. It's how you see it. In fact it's who you see them with. If you choose your Ego self you will experience trouble and resistance; if you choose to see it with the Holy Spirit you will see unification and love which will make you grateful. COVID-19 may have been terrible for the world, but for me it was a blessing as I helped my wife to raise our daughter together. I never missed a thing. To put it into context, babies go through different sleeping patterns. From birth it's pretty much continuous alongside feeding and nappy changes, there is no formal routine. We wanted a routine established so we could improve our sleeping patterns, so from five months we established three naps a day, then they dropped to two and then to one. Finally, when they are three to four years old or so, the day naps stop altogether as they prep for school. Guru-Je gave me the blessing of a task of putting the baby to bed. In that year she did not go to bed without me assisting her. She wanted her dad. It was at the three-a-day and two-a-day naps when Guru-

Je showed his magnificence and moved my meetings around. I remember I had an important call in 10 minutes' time as a board meeting, and I had the challenge to put her to sleep before it. That is change her nappy, comfort and rock her then transfer her to her cot (crib) and pat her until she was out. I gave it to the Holy Spirit and did it in six minutes flat, and made a coffee before the call. The world was in lockdown, and I was here juggling work, nappy changing, patting baby to sleep and caring for wife who was feeding the baby throughout the day. Towards the end of this lockdown Guru-Je sent more assistance as he wanted me to help work colleagues more with the skills he had given me. Two things happened. Firstly, the government introduced support bubbles for caring purposes so baby could now spend time with grandparents, secondly before the lockdown we only viewed one nursery and didn't have a chance to see others, but for the master that was all that was needed. The nursery was surprisingly open and many of our friends' nurseries nearby didn't reopen after the pandemic hit the nation.

I also became the head chef in the house as I wanted wife to have fresh food and it was Guru-Je who gave me images in my mind of the recipes to cook after work. Guru-Je took me under his abode and loved me unconditionally. I could feel that by handing everything over to the spirit I was using my Ego less and less, Akash was fading, and my real self was emerging as the covering was being removed. My motto was to serve, share and be open for direction. It's as close as we can be to what we are. Remember in the world of the Spirit we are telepathically connected to God automatically and it's in oneness that we create and extend together forever. Let's leave this chapter with the purpose of life. Rumi says, "Die before you die." He means remove the Ego self before the body dissolves. That way we close off the separated mind after the body ends, so we awaken inside of God and once there we only remember all of this as a little dream of nothing.

Solutions to Situations

Real Gratitude in every Situation

Love is the way I walk in gratitude. Gratitude is a lesson hard to learn for those who look upon the world amiss. The most that they can do is see themselves as better off than others. And they try to be content because another seems to suffer more than they. How pitiful and deprecating are such thoughts! For who has cause for thanks while others have less cause? And who could suffer less because he sees another suffer more? Your gratitude is due to Him alone Who made all cause of sorrow disappear throughout the world.

It is insane to offer thanks because of suffering. But it is equally insane to fail in gratitude to One Who offers you the certain means whereby all pain is healed, and suffering replaced with laughter and with happiness. Nor could the even partly sane refuse to take the steps which He directs, and follow in the way He sets before them, to escape a prison that they thought contained no door to the deliverance they now perceive.

Your brother is your "enemy" because you see in him the rival for your peace; a plunderer who takes his joy from you, and leaves you nothing but a black despair so bitter and relentless that there is no hope remaining. Now is vengeance all there is to wish for. Now can you but try to bring him down to lie in death with you, as useless as yourself; as little left within his grasping fingers as in yours.

You do not offer God your gratitude because your brother is more slave than you, nor could you sanely be enraged if he seems freer. Love makes no comparisons. And gratitude can only be sincere if it be joined to love. We offer thanks to God our Father that in us all things will find their freedom. It will never be that some are loosed while others still are bound. For who can bargain in the name of love?

Therefore give thanks, but in sincerity. And let your gratitude make room for all who will escape with you; the sick, the weak, the needy and afraid, and those who mourn a seeming loss or feel apparent pain, who suffer cold or hunger, or who walk the way of hatred and the path of death. All these go with you. Let us not compare ourselves with them, for thus we split them off from our awareness of the unity we share with them, as they must share with us.

We thank our Father for one thing alone; that we are separate from no living thing, and therefore one with Him. And we rejoice that no exceptions ever can be made which would reduce our wholeness, nor impair or change our function to complete the One Who is Himself completion. We give thanks for every living thing, for otherwise we offer thanks for nothing, and we fail to recognize the gifts of God to us.

Then let our brothers lean their tired heads against our shoulders as they rest a while. We offer thanks for them. For if we can direct them to the peace that we would find, the way is opening at last to us. An ancient door is swinging free again; a long forgotten Word re-echoes in our memory, and gathers clarity as we are willing once again to hear.

Walk, then, in gratitude the way of love. For hatred is forgotten when we lay comparisons aside. What more remains as obstacles to peace? The fear of God is now undone at last, and we forgive without comparing. Thus we cannot choose to overlook some things, and yet retain some other things still locked away as "sins." When your forgiveness is complete you will have total gratitude, for you will see that everything has earned the right to love by being loving, even as your Self.

Today we learn to think of gratitude in place of anger, malice and revenge. We have been given everything. If we refuse to recognize it, we are not entitled therefore to our bitterness, and to a self-perception which regards us in a place of merciless pursuit, where we are badgered ceaselessly, and pushed about without a thought or care for us or for our future. Gratitude becomes the single thought we substitute for these insane perceptions. God has cared for us, and calls us Son. Can there be more than this?

Our gratitude will pave the way to Him, and shorten our learning time by more than you could ever dream of. Gratitude goes hand in hand with love, and where one is the other must be found. For gratitude is but an aspect of the Love which is the Source of all creation. God gives thanks to you, His Son, for being what you are; His Own completion and the Source of love, along with Him. Your gratitude to Him is one with His to you. For love can walk no road except the way of gratitude, and thus we go who walk the way to God. (W-P1.195.1:1)

If we are completely honest with ourselves, we're very likely to have done this many times in our life and most of us continue to do it now as it's habitual. We hear of the sufferings others face and count our blessings that it is not us in that situation. This is so normal in our world. If you see a homeless person with no shelter, money or food we may help them, but deep down are grateful that it is not us in that position. When a friend's child is born, and we see them suffer more with diseases, conditions, or body impairments we feel for them but are grateful that our child doesn't go through that. When a close friend's home gets burgled at knifepoint, we comfort and support them but inside our ego mind is grateful that that's not our experience. When other elderly people become sick and weak, we look at our parents' activeness and feel grateful for this. Some of us call that luck, fortune or fate. Others thank God it's not happened to them. But which God are you thanking because the creator of all blesses some and not others? Our mind is so conditioned to see suffering as true that we don't actually "see" what is there. Jesus calls these thoughts "pitiful and deprecating" as how can we be thankful while others have less? And who could suffer less because he sees another suffer more? True gratitude is owed directly to God our creator who made all the cause of unhappiness, sadness and grief disappear all over the world. It's impossible that some of us are blessed more than others as love is whole and can't be bargained with. Gratitude is to our creator who gave us a guaranteed way where all pain is healed, and suffering replaced with laughter and happiness. To be so grateful to him that he held the kingdom for us in a perfect oneness state and didn't acknowledge our thought of separating from him, so actually this is only a dream not a "real separation". We are thankful to our Father God that in us all things will find their freedom. When we feel gratitude there is humility that somebody has helped us, taught us or given us something that we feel grateful for. Therefore we are also grateful to the Holy Spirit and its manifestations of Jesus, Guruji and other elder brothers whom we respect and love very dearly. Within the deep darkness of this world, where guilt emerges around every corner, pain and discomfort follows us throughout life, when we feel trapped into oblivion, our gratitude is that we have been saved, rescued from the Ego's pits of misery by the Holy Spirit. Gratitude also comes to all the other parts of you who allow you the opportunity to see through the veil in front of them to reveal the real universal being in them which is all of us. By them appearing as they are not, you can see them as they are and thus see your true self. How grateful to them must we surely be for that. They are showing us what's in our mind so we can clear it out through forgiveness, otherwise we would surely be lost here. It's this humble gratitude that we walk home with each other which is total love. We are also grateful for *A Course in Miracles* for giving the knowledge of our truth back to us thus removing the veil of forgetfulness.

Trying to Help yourself

When I first started the course, I had a feeling that I seemed to know a secret that not many others knew. One of the emotions I felt was arrogance through "trying to help" as the Ego crept in and made me believe "I" needed to help out. At the start I knew nothing about the Ego's tricks and was still establishing a trustworthy relationship with the Holy Spirit. "You need do nothing" was not completely understood as all my life I've always decided for "myself" what to do. It's this self that intrudes on the holy relationship between you and the Holy Spirit. We tend to look for the answer, but we must receive the answer as it is given. As I was trying very hard to find the Holy instant which is "now" I was trying to make myself holy to receive it, but that's not my role, that's God's. It's arrogance to try to prepare for holiness and believe that it is up to me to establish the conditions for peace. God has established them; the conditions do not wait for my willingness for what they are.

If I felt I was unworthy of learning this, then I was simply interfering.

Trust not your good intentions. They are not enough. But trust implicitly your willingness, whatever else may enter. Concentrate only on this and be not disturbed that shadows surround it. That is why you came. If you could come without them, you would not need the holy instant. Come to it not in arrogance, assuming that you must achieve the state its coming brings with it. The miracle of the holy instant lies in your willingness to let it be what it is. And in your willingness for this lies also your acceptance of yourself as you were meant to be.

Humility will never ask that you remain content with littleness. But it does require that you be not content with less than greatness that comes not of you. Your difficulty with the holy instant arises from your fixed conviction that you are not worthy of it. And what is this but the determination to be as you would make yourself? God did not create his dwelling place unworthy of him. And if you believe he cannot enter where he wills to be, you must be interfering with his will. You do not need the strength of willingness to come from you, but only from his will. (T-18.4.2:1)

We make way for the undoing of the Ego. We don't do it, that's the Holy Spirit's role. Purification is from God for you. I do not interfere with his plan to restore my own awareness of my readiness, which is eternal. I need add nothing to his plan. Just Surrender fully and that is only the little that is asked. Give him what he asks, so we can learn how little is our part, and how great is his. Remember we made guilt, and that our plan for the escape from guilt has been to bring undoing to it and make salvation fearful. And it is only fear that we will add if we prepare ourselves for love. Let's not forget that it has been our decision to make everything that is natural and easy for us impossible. At the start we believe the entering into the present moment is difficult but everything God wills is not only possible but has already happened. And that is why the past has gone. It never happened in reality. Only in our dreams.

Trying to Help Others

When we learn more through the course it's natural to try to assist others with this new information. But I remember when I was very Ego centered. I never wanted to listen to the spiritual people as I thought I knew best for myself which is arrogance, but is it not also arrogance to try to think we know best of others? We must respect their mind, if they choose the Ego wrong mindedness now it's also the same mind that will choose the Holy Spirit's right mindedness one day. Jesus has infinite patience because the outcome is certain that we will choose right one day and be in God's mind.

Let's ensure we don't deprive others of their mistakes. It's their classroom the same way we learnt our own to be where we are now.

Correcting others

Correcting others is the Holy Spirit's job, not yours. It's not for you to act superior and tell others what to do. The Ego wants you to point out errors and "correct" them but it's unaware of what errors are and what correction is. When you correct your brother, you are telling him he is wrong. He may be making no sense at the time and it is certain that if he is speaking from the Ego he will not be making sense but your task is still to tell him he is right. You do not tell him this verbally. If he is speaking foolishly, he needs correction at another level, because his error is at another level. He is still right because he is a Child of God. His Ego is always wrong no matter what it says or does. If you point out errors of your brother's Ego you must be seeing it through yours because the Holy Spirit does not perceive his errors. This must be true since there is no communication between the Ego and Holy Spirit. When you react at all to errors, you are not listening to the Holy Spirit. If you do not hear him you are listening to your Ego; by not listening to him you are making as little sense as the brother whose errors you perceive. Any attempt you make to correct another means that you believe correction by you is possible, and this can only be the arrogance of the Ego. Correction is of God who does not know of arrogance. So, what do we actually do here? Stop and hear your brother with the Holy Spirit. Remember however he is acting he is God's Child. Verbally do not correct him – notice it, don't analyze it as that will be of the Ego and making it real. Remove all judgments. Forgive what you Incorrectly perceive with your mind, not verbally. Correction is done of God. Forgive what your brother has not done.

Generosity and patience

To the world, generosity means "giving away" in the sense of "giving up". To the teachers of God, it means giving away in order to keep. The teacher of God does not want anything he cannot give away, because he realizes it would be valueless to him by definition. What would he want it for? He could only lose because of it. He could not gain. Therefore, he does not seek what only he could keep, because that is a guarantee of loss. He does not want to suffer.

Those who are certain of the outcome can afford to wait and wait without anxiety. Patience is natural to the teacher of God. All he sees is certain outcome, at a time perhaps unknown to him yet, but not in doubt. The time will be as right as is the answer.

I am here to be truly helpful / What is healing

I regularly say, *"I am here to be truly helpful,"* to myself at work, at funerals, when someone is unable to move much and needs assistance, when someone has a disease and knows death is close, or any situation when assistance is required. I recently assisted my mother in a garden party, my brother and wife couldn't attend due to a last-minute situation, so I completely offered myself to arrive early and help in whatever way spirit wanted to express love. It came up with all sorts of ideas, to cut limes and strawberries finely and put onto the side of champagne glasses, to go directly to the guests (who were my mum's friends and I didn't really know) and make sure they have a drink, to dance with Mum, set up the music for the party vibe, cut the cake with timed music and serve champagne, and my favorite was talking to complete strangers which are actually telling me what's in my mind and one I had to forgive also for giving me the interpretation that having a shaved head wasn't attractive. Serving through humility and humbleness occurs when you know you don't need anything to make you more complete because you are immortal. Below is what the course says about being truly helpful.

I am here only to be truly helpful.
I am here to represent him who sent me.

I do not have to worry about what to say or what to do, because he who sent me will direct me.
I am content to be wherever he wishes, knowing he goes there with me.
I will be healed as I let Him teach me to heal. (T-2.6.8:3)

After reading this, it's very useful to next understand what healing is.

This question really answers itself. Healing cannot be repeated. If the patient is healed, what remains to heal him from? And if the healing is certain, as we have already said it is, what is there to repeat? For a teacher of God to remain concerned about the result of healing is to limit the healing. It is now the teacher of God himself whose mind needs to be healed. And it is this he must facilitate. He is now the patient, and he must so regard himself. He has made a mistake, and must be willing to change his mind about it. He lacked the trust that makes for giving truly, and so he has not received the benefit of his gift.

Whenever a teacher of God has tried to be a channel for healing he has succeeded. Should he be tempted to doubt this, he should not repeat his previous effort. That was already maximal, because the Holy Spirit so accepted it and so used it. Now the teacher of God has only one course to follow. He must use his reason to tell himself that he has given the problem to One Who cannot fail, and must recognize that his own uncertainty is not love but fear, and therefore hate. His position has thus become untenable, for he is offering hate to one to whom he offered love. This is impossible. Having offered love, only love can be received.

It is in this that the teacher of God must trust. This is what is really meant by the statement that the one responsibility of the miracle worker is to accept the Atonement for himself. The teacher of God is a miracle worker because he gives the gifts he has received. Yet he must first accept them. He need do no more, nor is there more that he could do. By accepting healing he can give it. If he doubts this, let him remember Who gave the gift and Who received it. Thus is his doubt corrected. He thought the gifts of God could be withdrawn. That was a mistake, but hardly one to stay with. And so the teacher of God can only recognize it for what it is, and let it be corrected for him.

One of the most difficult temptations to recognize is that to doubt a healing because of the appearance of continuing symptoms is a mistake in the form of lack of trust. As such it is an attack. Usually it seems to be just the opposite. It does appear unreasonable at first to be told that continued concern is attack. It has all the appearances of love. Yet love without trust is impossible, and doubt and trust cannot coexist. And hate must be the opposite of love, regardless of the form it takes. Doubt not the gift and it is impossible to doubt its result. This is the certainty that gives God's teachers the power to be miracle workers, for they have put their trust in Him.

The real basis for doubt about the outcome of any problem that has been given to God's Teacher for resolution is always self-doubt. And that necessarily implies that trust has been placed in an illusory self, for only such a self can be doubted. This illusion can take many forms. Perhaps there is a fear of weakness and vulnerability. Perhaps there is a fear of failure and shame associated with a sense of inadequacy. Perhaps there is a guilty embarrassment stemming from false humility. The form of the mistake is not important. What is important is only the recognition of a mistake as a mistake. The mistake is always some form of concern with the self to the exclusion of the patient. It is a failure to recognize him as part of the Self, and thus represents a confusion in identity. Conflict about what you are has entered your mind, and you have become deceived about yourself. And you are deceived about yourself because you have denied the Source of your creation. If you are offering only healing, you cannot doubt. If you really want the problem solved, you cannot doubt. If you are certain what the problem is, you cannot doubt. Doubt is the result of conflicting wishes. Be sure of what you want, and doubt becomes impossible. (M-7.1.1:1)

Healing is not done by you, it's done of you. You can't heal yourself, but you can allow yourself to be healed by the Holy Spirit. At the very start of the course when trust is being built still with the Holy Spirit and the Ego still seemed to have some power over me, I was definitely in a position when I doubted healing sometimes and had a lack of trust. This is because I couldn't always see the healing happen in form which is what Jesus is saying here with the "appearance of continued symptoms". Jesus is saying here that this is lack of trust so, *"Doubt not the gift and it is impossible to doubt its result. This is the certainty that gives God's teachers the power to be miracle workers, for they have put their trust in Him."* It's very important to never forget what you are and what the other is. The Child of God, we may think this is arrogance, but have you ever thought that the real arrogance here is that we think we can change ourselves from being God's eternal changeless creation. We have created this "person" and we have done this before as many lives. The Ego presents many ways to stop us joining through the miracle by a sense of inadequacy, fear of failure, weakness, or guilty embarrassment. Removing all the doubts and putting full trust in this will result in your entire outside world becoming peaceful, I assure you.

Messenger

I wanted to put this in this book because it has been such a great help to me in tricky situations. I work in a friendly environment; however, I have executive board meetings twice a month to be a part of which isn't always friendly. On the level of form these members are my bosses' bosses and also include the ultimate boss, the company's chief executive. As I first started the course, I was also starting this job at the same time. This job was given to me by Guruji as my classroom of learning. At the beginning this job role was quite daunting but I had the course to guide me through it. There were stages when I felt a lack in me for these obvious worldly reasons; I was much lower in hierarchy than other members, my role wasn't as large as these other leaders, so my knowledge exposure was less than theirs. There's also the authority situation and also the ages of all of these people are 60+ where I was coming closer to 37. There was also another twist; my boss wasn't a member of this board, his boss was. Which meant I had to involve him, or he would feel undermined. There have been many times when I have had to present detailed figures to the board, respond to challenging questions and be crystal clear on the message. This of course makes me the messenger. And Jesus puts this so clearly in the course. I literally give him the body as a host and he flows through me with thoughts, words and even the board members' words are guided by him (Jesus says I inspire miracles). He is setting the entire scene up so I can deliver the message he wants. There are some board meetings that I have not said a single thing, but others where I'm the main character. The truth here also is there's no hierarchy to illusions, only a constant state of oneness exists. They are not really superior to me in any way as I'm actually just talking to myself due to there being no one else out there, a lack in me can't exist as I was created by God, age doesn't exist as our being is ageless and although their superficial knowledge seemed greater we all share the only truth of knowledge there is, as spirit. This passage has and still will get me through these ego entanglements:

Let us today be neither arrogant nor falsely humble. We have gone beyond such foolishness. We cannot judge ourselves, nor need we do so. These are but attempts to hold decision off, and to delay commitment to our function. It is not our part to judge our worth, nor can we know what role is best for us; what we can do within a larger plan we cannot see in its entirety. Our part is cast in Heaven, not in hell. And what we think is weakness can be strength; what

209

we believe to be our strength is often arrogance.

Whatever your appointed role may be, it was selected by the Voice for God, Whose function is to speak for you as well. Seeing your strengths exactly as they are, and equally aware of where they can be best applied, for what, to whom and when, He chooses and accepts your part for you. He does not work without your own consent. But He is not deceived in what you are, and listens only to His Voice in you.

It is through His ability to hear one Voice which is His Own that you become aware at last there is one Voice in you. And that one Voice appoints your function, and relays it to you, giving you the strength to understand it, do what it entails, and to succeed in everything you do that is related to it. God has joined His Son in this, and thus His Son becomes His messenger of unity with Him. It is this joining, through the Voice for God, of Father and of Son, that sets apart salvation from the world. It is this Voice which speaks of laws the world does not obey; which promises salvation from all sin, with guilt abolished in the mind that God created sinless. Now this mind becomes aware again of Who created it, and of His lasting union with itself. So is its Self the one reality in which its will and that of God are joined.

A messenger is not the one who writes the message he delivers. Nor does he question the right of him who does, nor ask why he has chosen those who will receive the message that he brings. It is enough that he accept it, give it to the ones for whom it is intended, and fulfill his role in its delivery. If he determines what the messages should be, or what their purpose is, or where they should be carried, he is failing to perform his proper part as bringer of the Word.

There is one major difference in the role of Heaven's messengers, which sets them off from those the world appoints. The messages that they deliver are intended first for them. And it is only as they can accept them for themselves that they become able to bring them further, and to give them everywhere that they were meant to be.

Like earthly messengers, they did not write the messages they bear, but they become their first receivers in the truest sense, receiving to prepare themselves to give.

An earthly messenger fulfills his role by giving all his messages away. The messengers of God perform their part by their acceptance of His messages as for themselves, and show they understand the messages by giving them away. They choose no roles that are not given them by His authority. And so they gain by every message that they give away.

Would you receive the messages of God? For thus do you become His messenger. You are appointed now. And yet you wait to give the messages you have received. And so you do not know that they are yours, and do not recognize them. No one can receive and understand he has received until he gives. For in the giving is his own acceptance of what he received.

You who are now the messenger of God, receive His messages. For that is part of your appointed role. God has not failed to offer what you need, nor has it been left unaccepted. Yet another part of your appointed task is yet to be accomplished. He Who has received for you the messages of God would have them be received by you as well. For thus do you identify with Him and claim your own.

It is this joining that we undertake to recognize today. We will not seek to keep our minds apart from Him Who speaks for us, for it is but our voice we hear as we attend Him. He alone can speak to us and for us, joining in one Voice the getting and the giving of God's Word; the giving and receiving of His Will.

We practice giving Him what He would have, that we may recognize His gifts to us. He needs our voice that He may speak through us. He needs our hands to hold His messages, and carry them to those whom He appoints. He needs our feet to bring us where He wills, that those who wait in misery may be at last delivered. And He needs our will united with His Own, that we may be the true receivers of the gifts He gives.

Let us but learn this lesson for today: We will not recognize what

*we receive until we give it. You have heard this said a hundred
ways, a hundred times, and yet belief is lacking still. But this is
sure; until belief is given it, you will receive a thousand miracles
and then receive a thousand more, but will not know that God
Himself has left no gift beyond what you already have; nor has
denied the tiniest of blessings to His Son. What can this mean to
you, until you have identified with Him and with His Own? Our
lesson for today is stated thus:*

*I am among the ministers of God, and I am grateful that I have the
means by which to recognize that I am free.*

*The world recedes as we light up our minds, and realize these holy
words are true. They are the message sent to us today from our
Creator. Now we demonstrate how they have changed our minds
about ourselves, and what our function is. For as we prove that we
accept no will we do not share, our many gifts from our Creator
will spring to our sight and leap into our hands, and we will
recognize what we received.* (W-P1.154.1:1)

A Trip to the Temple – Strong Debate Situations

I recently decided to go to the Hare Krishna Temple in Watford as
my little toddler likes the cows and ducks there, and since on the
surface our dream figures are Hindu it's a great way to introduce
her to Lord Krishna. We went into the Temple and showed our
gratitude to the Deities, ate the delicious prasad (which are
vegetarian offerings to Lord Krishna first) and enjoyed the new
children's playground built there recently. As I sat down and
watched my little one play, a monk who teaches the Bhagavad
Gita came over and said hi to me. We engaged into a very deep
discussion on *A Course in Miracles* and Krishna Consciousness.
There were lots of similarities. He calls the world Maya, the course
refers to it as an illusionary world or a dream. He said we have
slight independence here which we miscreate, and the course talks
about this with following the Ego thought system. We agreed on
everything but there was one thing he didn't agree with at all. That

Oneness is the supreme goal. He said we all live together as souls within Krishna's abode in Gokula. I said souls imply separateness which we can never be with our creator. We debated this quite strongly, as I had one eye on my daughter playing as well. I closed it off with we don't know what oneness is as it's a state beyond where we are with experiences and words, but together we are in that state when time is over. This conversation was quite an unexpected strong debate. It wasn't a light gentle discussion, and I felt it being pushed onto me. I forgave him immediately as it felt uneasy, and the Holy Spirit seemed to be talking through my toddler very loudly telling me repeatedly she wanted to go to see the cows now and directing me away from the conversation. So, I said my goodbyes, we got our things together and went to the cows. I put the pram (stroller) away, and carried her in my arm so she could see the cows close up. Another child and dad were next to us, and I was talking to the dad about children's stuff and my daughter said, "Daddy, Daddy." I was still talking to the other dad and then she said, "Daddy, Daddy, look one home" – I turned to her shocked and asked her to repeat it. When she said, "look one home," she was referring to the only cow in front of her who happened to have one horn. But this was the Holy Spirit confirming that whatever we want to call it, and however we want to describe it – it's one home for all of us with God and that's not here in this world which is a dream. I was very thankful to the monk as bringer of this gift. The clarification of terms in the course describes this about the word "soul":

> *Spirit is the part that is still in contact with God through the Holy Spirit, Who abides in this part but sees the other part as well. The term "soul" is not used except in direct biblical quotations because of its highly controversial nature. It would, however, be an equivalent of "spirit," with the understanding that, being of God, it is eternal and was never born.* (CL-1.3)

Epilogue

We all arrive to this book at different stages on our journey. Some want a closer relationship with the higher self. Some don't know what *A Course in Miracles* is and maybe this is their introduction to it. Others may be course students looking for a new lens to see the course from, and some may be Guruji followers looking to explore his encounters with me. For whatever the reason is, inward peace will be the conclusion if we follow forgiveness with the Holy Spirit, Jesus, Guruji: the Non-Ego Part of ourselves.

I wanted to Thank you for connecting with me on this journey. For some of you this is likely to have not been easy as lots of the knowledge in this book aims to dismantle the beliefs we had before this book arrived. We have been educated to accept separation between each other, but as we unwind our perception back, the realization that we are the same arises. When we look for the real self, we naturally first look for a solid and amazing self, but as each belief we hold about the self-identity is interrogated, we find that what we are looking for is not self-existence. It's dissolving into pure existence and leads to nothing. This nothing is the beginning of everything. To the Ego this sounds dreadful, but as borders disappear, I ask you the question: do you know where your mind starts and ends? The answer you will now know: there is one mind within the whole universe, and this includes your mind. This leads to living a life of all inclusiveness as you see yourself in all beings.

Together we can shift our collective consciousness to divinity and peace. The course is an excellent tool to follow. I really admire *how* Jesus teaches us. It's gentle but unwavering, and what he does is uncover what the entire Ego thought system is about. The problem is not what the Ego does, but that we are not mindful of what the Ego does. Therefore, I'm not surprised the Ego chapter became the largest in this book to help you with what it hides. The Ego does nothing, but we think it is something and therefore Jesus shows us it is nothing. Equally as vital, Jesus also shows us why we are so invested in thinking the Ego is something and that what the Ego does is something that demands attention. So, Jesus unveils the Ego. He shows us that its answer doesn't work, then demonstrates that the issue this answer is addressing doesn't exist, and finally shows us the place where this problem is supposed to exist doesn't exist either, for there is no time or world.

Connecting to Guruji is Godsend. He is so practical with life and has wonderful ways to show me he's always here, very subtly. Just this morning my toddler had my wallet on the floor, and she was trying to eat all the coins that dropped out. A choking hazard as they call it. I had a slight wish that I could not have so much change in my wallet to weigh my pockets down and stop my little one having too much fun with the coins. I took her to Marks & Spencer's to give her a ride in the trolly, she loves to explore the aisles. As I parked and was taking her out of the car seat, a man passes me and says, "Brother, please can you spare some change." I said, "It's only coppers I'm afraid." He said, "Every little leads to eating." I took that as referring to my little one eating the coins but it also means him getting some food of course. I giggled to myself because Guruji was saying hi in his own way. Now what will really get you thinking here is, did he actually give me the money exchange experience, or did he just give me the interpretation of it? I'll leave that with you.

Love to Guruji's entire Sangat Following.
Love to all fellow *A Course in Miracle* affiliates.
Love to everyone else who is equally joined with me in every other way.

Copyright Acknowledgments

All quotes are from *A Course in Miracles*, copyright ©1992, 1999, 2007 by the Foundation for Inner Peace, 448 Ignacio Blvd., #306, Novato, CA 94949, www.acim.org and info@acim.org, used with permission.

All page numbers are for the Public Domain version of *A Course in Miracles* found at:

http://stobblehouse.com/text/ACIM.pdf.

ACIM Annotation System for referencing text

T Text
W Workbook For Students
M Manual for Teachers
CL Clarification of Terms

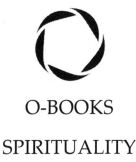

O-BOOKS

SPIRITUALITY

O is a symbol of the world, of oneness and unity; this eye
represents knowledge and insight. We publish titles on general
spirituality and living a spiritual life. We aim to inform and help
you on your own journey in this life.
If you have enjoyed this book, why not tell other readers by
posting a review on your preferred book site?

Recent bestsellers from O-Books are:

Heart of Tantric Sex
Diana Richardson
Revealing Eastern secrets of deep love and intimacy to Western
couples.
Paperback: 978-1-90381-637-0 ebook: 978-1-84694-637-0

Crystal Prescriptions
The A-Z guide to over 1,200 symptoms and their healing crystals
Judy Hall
The first in the popular series of eight books, this handy little
guide is packed as tight as a pill-bottle with crystal remedies for
ailments.
Paperback: 978-1-90504-740-6 ebook: 978-1-84694-629-5

Your Simple Path
Find Happiness in every step
Ian Tucker
A guide to helping us reconnect with what is really important in
our lives.
Paperback: 978-1-78279-349-6 ebook: 978-1-78279-348-9

365 Days of Wisdom
Daily Messages To Inspire You Through The Year
Dadi Janki
Daily messages which cool the mind, warm the heart and guide
you along your journey.
Paperback: 978-1-84694-863-3 ebook: 978-1-84694-864-0

Body of Wisdom
Women's Spiritual Power and How it Serves
Hilary Hart
Bringing together the dreams and experiences of women across
the world with today's most visionary spiritual teachers.
Paperback: 978-1-78099-696-7 ebook: 978-1-78099-695-0

Dying to Be Free
From Enforced Secrecy to Near Death to True Transformation
Hannah Robinson
After an unexpected accident and near-death experience, Hannah
Robinson found herself radically transforming her life, while a
remarkable new insight altered her relationship with her father, a
practising Catholic priest.
Paperback: 978-1-78535-254-6 ebook: 978-1-78535-255-3

The Ecology of the Soul
A Manual of Peace, Power and Personal Growth for Real People
in the Real World
Aidan Walker
Balance your own inner Ecology of the Soul to regain your
natural state of peace, power and wellbeing.
Paperback: 978-1-78279-850-7 ebook: 978-1-78279-849-1

Not I, Not other than I
The Life and Teachings of Russel Williams
Steve Taylor, Russel Williams
The miraculous life and inspiring teachings of one of the World's
greatest living Sages.
Paperback: 978-1-78279-729-6 ebook: 978-1-78279-728-9

On the Other Side of Love
A woman's unconventional journey towards wisdom
Muriel Maufroy
When life has lost all meaning, what do you do?
Paperback: 978-1-78535-281-2 ebook: 978-1-78535-282-9

Practicing A Course In Miracles
A translation of the Workbook in plain language, with
mentor's notes
Elizabeth A. Cronkhite
The practical second and third volumes of The Plain-Language
A Course In Miracles.
Paperback: 978-1-84694-403-1 ebook: 978-1-78099-072-9

Quantum Bliss
The Quantum Mechanics of Happiness, Abundance, and Health
George S. Mentz
Quantum Bliss is the breakthrough summary of success and spirituality secrets that customers have been waiting for.
Paperback: 978-1-78535-203-4 ebook: 978-1-78535-204-1

The Upside Down Mountain
Mags MacKean
A must-read for anyone weary of chasing success and happiness – one woman's inspirational journey swapping the uphill slog for the downhill slope.
Paperback: 978-1-78535-171-6 ebook: 978-1-78535-172-3

Your Personal Tuning Fork
The Endocrine System
Deborah Bates
Discover your body's health secret, the endocrine system, and 'twang' your way to sustainable health!
Paperback: 978-1-84694-503-8 ebook: 978-1-78099-697-4

Readers of ebooks can buy or view any of these bestsellers by clicking on the live link in the title. Most titles are published in paperback and as an ebook. Paperbacks are available in traditional bookshops. Both print and ebook formats are available online.
Find more titles and sign up to our readers' newsletter at
http://www.johnhuntpublishing.com/mind-body-spirit
Follow us on Facebook at https://www.facebook.com/OBooks/
and Twitter at https://twitter.com/obooks